Reframing

*A Systems Thinking Look at
IT Service Management*

Steve Hales

with Patrick Hoverstadt
and Tony Korycki

ITIL® is a (registered) Trade Mark of AXELOS Limited. All rights reserved.

Authors

Steve Hales worked for seven years on large outsourced IT accounts for EDS and then HP in both the public and private sectors. He has worked as an internal change and organisational design consultant, interim change manager and a service support process architect – he is an ITIL Expert. Steve is also a practitioner of the viable system model and a director of SCiO (Systems and Complexity in Organisation) – a business educational charity supporting practitioners using systems thinking approaches. Steve trained originally as an environmental biochemist and worked with Unilever. He can be contacted at ITILreframe@halesemail.net.

Patrick Hoverstadt is a consultant focusing on organisational design, strategy, business architecture and organisational change using systems approaches. He has developed a set of methodologies that provide different approaches for organisational change, performance management, strategic risk, strategy, partnership governance and organisational agility. He is a director of SCiO and is the author of The Fractal Organisation (Wiley, 2009) and co-author of Patterns of Strategy (Gower, 2016). He does some academic work for Manchester Business School and the OU and is a visiting research fellow at Cranfield. He can be contacted at patrick@fractal-consulting.com.

Tony Korycki is a specialist in organisational improvement, including leadership and management of change. Tony has 25 years of experience in systems thinking, measurements, benchmarking, quality, and as a process architect for ITIL request and change processes, most recently in BT's Global Services business. Tony is a director of SCiO and of the Deming Alliance, supporting practitioners using systems thinking approaches. He is currently studying for the OU's postgraduate qualification in Systems Thinking. He can be contacted at tonykorycki@hotmail.com.

Acknowledgements

I would like to thank Patrick Hoverstadt and Tony Korycki – both of SCiO (Systems and Complexity in Organisation) who worked with me on many occasions to develop the systems approaches to ITIL described here and to carry out detailed analyses – especially for Chapter 6 – and resolve confusions. I would also like to thank Paul Billany, Paul Brayford, Ian Glossop, Philip Hellyer, Dot Tudor and Rob Young (also all of SCiO) for their contributions, suggestions, reviews and comments. Thanks also to Rob Worth for his help with editing and proofreading. Part of the preparation of this book was carried out through a SCiO Common Interest Group (CIG). All errors and stylistic oddities are mine.

Steve Hales – January 2020

Disclaimer

The issues with implementation of ITIL and IT Service Management that are discussed in this book are based on experience and observation of a wide range of IT support organisations. Most have been observed many times and it is our belief that they are widespread throughout the sector.

Please help

The focus of *Reframing ITIL* is derived from the experience of the authors and their collaborators. However, we are well aware that many areas could be expanded with more experience – particularly Agile, DevOps, SIAM and multi client service providers – and invite you to contact us with your experiences – whether they reinforce or contradict our observations. Any additional thoughts or examples for other sections are also welcomed. As ITIL 4 is rolled out and experience gained, we would again welcome your observations. We will endeavour to incorporate some of these into future editions with full accreditation should you wish it. Please send comments to ITILreframe@halesemail.net .

SCiO

SCiO (Systems and Complexity in Organisation) is a community of systems thinking practitioners in the UK and elsewhere who believe that traditional approaches to running organisations are responsible for many of the problems we see today. We believe that systemic approaches to designing and running organisations offer radically new and better alternatives.

SCiO has three main objectives:

- Developing practice in applying systems ideas to a range of organisational issues
- Disseminating the use of systems approaches in dealing with organisational issues
- Supporting practitioners in their professional practice

Please see our website for more details – www.systemspractice.org.

Contents

Preface i

Introduction iii

1. Supporting the Service 1
2. Organising to Support the Service 23
3. Developing the Service 43
4. Managing the Service 61
5. Managing the Service Organisation 79
6. Designing the Service Organisation 95
7. Outsourcing the Service 129
8. Summary 153

Further Reading 165

Preface

This book is for readers who already have some familiarity with ITIL and/or work in IT service organisations. It will be useful for managers, consultants, ITIL specialists and trainers to provide context and solutions to everyday problems of planning, organising and implementing ITIL. It is rooted in version 3 of ITIL as that is what we have all been using for the past decade (although there have been traces of ITIL 2 around in some organisations for much of that time!). The main difference with ITIL 4 is the refocus of the operating model and introduction of the Service Value System but the core of ITIL is still there and most of the points introduced in this book are still going to be relevant. Once there are a few years' experience of ITIL 4, it will be possible to re-examine it.

This is something of a Marmite book based on the reactions we have so far received. If you like ideas and overviews and strategy and how things work – then this book is for you! If you prefer detailed processes and specifications, then you might be disappointed.

ITIL has been used in IT Service Management for a couple of decades now, but despite this, not all implementations deliver the expected value. Managers also frequently don't understand ITIL's importance or significance. This book is based on the principle that you can't manage something you don't understand and is intended to enhance your understanding of how ITIL and IT Service Management work. This is done with mainly visual 'frames' to make it accessible.

The frames show how ITIL processes work – individually and together – and how the combination produces IT Service Management organisations. Most of these frames are heavily influenced by a systems thinking approach – many based in the viable system model.

One of the biggest problems for users of ITIL is the piecemeal way it is often trained, introduced and delivered. By understanding the whole picture, ITIL managers, consultants, trainers and users can see where a particular implementation is likely to be effective or go wrong.

This book is not an introduction to ITIL; in some ways it is a critique of ITIL, but that is not its purpose. On the contrary it is to show where and how ITIL does work and where and how it is not quite there yet. Overall ITIL is a very effective framework and using the processes and standards it provides can be an extremely effective way of improving the quality of IT support in any organisation.

Introduction

Do we need ITIL?
ITIL was developed to provide a standard approach to IT service management to improve government commissioning of IT services from third parties. It was taken up fairly enthusiastically by a number of large, private-sector, IT service providers. ITIL makes it far easier for standard approaches to be taken to managing IT services by providers of all types. In turn, this makes it easier to commission IT services for the client business. ITIL makes it easier to transfer staff from one IT service provider to another, whether service management is being outsourced or transferred from one provider to another. For the individual, it makes it much easier to move from one provider to another. All of these things remain true pretty much whether ITIL is good or indifferent (but perhaps not if it is bad…).

Over the years, ITIL has gone through a number of iterations both large and small and its scope has slowly changed to incorporate the whole management of an IT services business. This is more a matter of change of emphasis than scope, but that change of emphasis has been substantial – moving from a focus on the operational side of service management (ITIL and ITIL 2) to the wider context of the IT services business (ITIL 3 on...). The latest iteration, ITIL 4, again revisits this. The implementation of ITIL by many service providers has not entirely followed this change – perhaps ITIL has overstepped its natural domain?

The authors and their collaborators have been involved in organisations using ITIL processes in service management and have observed the benefits and problems of ITIL implementations of various types – including partial implementations and varying interpretations. They have applied systems approaches to IT service management and identified patterns and omissions which may be helpful in guiding more successful implementations.

The ITIL frame
In this book we are going to look at how implementing ITIL can help (or hinder) service management to deliver effectively. We are going to look at how the ITIL processes relate to one another – and especially what sort of processes they are. Also we are going to look at how the ITIL processes fit into organisations: initially into standardised organisations, and then a variety of

Reframing ITIL

real organisational types. For readers who like patterns and structures, this should make understanding how ITIL works, far easier. The organisational model we will use is the viable system model and is a fundamental component of systems thinking, so by stealth the reader will be introduced to a new way of thinking about ITIL and organisations which may have additional value!

This book is based in ITIL 3 and the terminology used is ITIL 3 terminology. However, based on an early reading of ITIL 4 we do not believe that any of the fundamental points made will change. A diagram has been used throughout the book that shows the ITIL processes grouped according to the five 'books' or disciplines of ITIL 3: Service Operation, Service Transition, Service Design, Service Strategy and Continual Service Improvement. This frame sets a context for the discussions of each chapter that is focused on processes (namely Chapters 1-5). It is likely that most of you will be far more familiar with this context than the ITIL 4 structure as we first publish this.

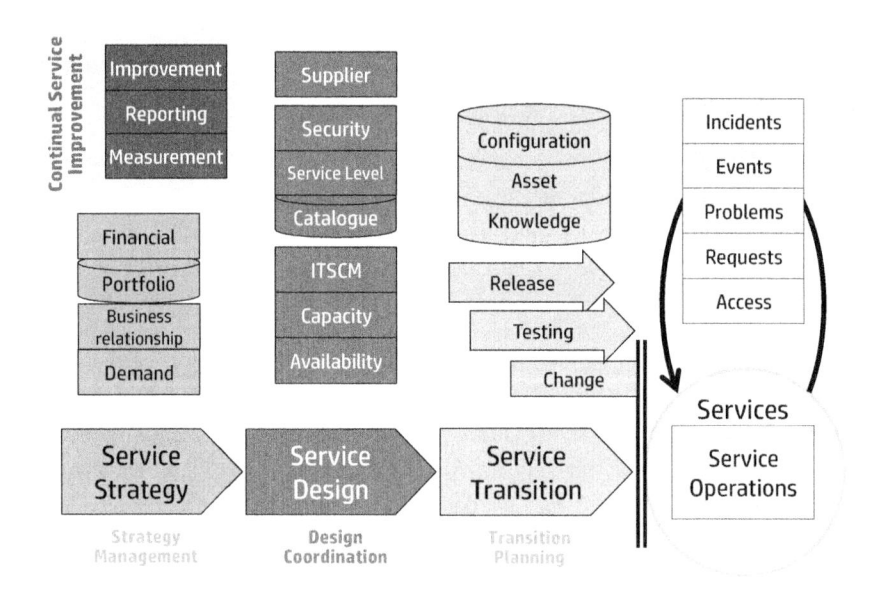

Figure – ITIL processes grouped by the five disciplines of ITIL 3

Definition of a service

ITIL is about delivering services to businesses and other types of organisation. It is therefore worth briefly discussing services before embarking on our investigation of IT Service Management and ITIL: Broadly speaking there are two types of organisations – those that make widgets and those that provide services.

If an organisation makes a widget we know clearly that its primary activity is manufacturing widgets. By way of contrast, selling the widget, servicing the widget, fixing, enhancing or replacing the widget would never be confused with widget making even if they are done by different parts of the same organisation. These are usually called 'supporting services' and this does not confuse them with making the widget. Imagine for example that the widget is a car and this becomes clearer.

However, if an organisation provides a service as its primary activity, then it is not uncommon to call every other activity – selling the service, managing the service, fixing the service, enhancing or replacing the service – which the organisation carries out, a service as well. Confusion begins to reign! Even the processes used to do this can be called services. It is very important that we define the primary activity – provision of the service – as the service and see everything else in relation to this.

Bearing this definition of the service in mind, most organisations clearly have a substantial part of their activities dedicated to delivering (as opposed to developing or supporting) the service. Except that in IT, this part of the operation may actually be quite a small activity in isolation because much of the 'provision' is automated (see later in Chapter 3): Imagine the provision of email – it is all done by bits of software communicating with one another on different servers and computers located in many different places. Noone collects emails from a post box, noone has to deliver them by hand. The actual provision of the service is automatic and is physical resource heavy, but not human resource heavy.

In fact, there is a lot of activity to ensure a service is delivered, but it tends to be in dealing with issues – many proactively before the user is aware. Some activity is preventative, as in making sure backups take place. So the activity is at a lower level and ensures that the service is functioning properly rather than delivering the service in itself.

It should be noted that there are exceptions to this – even today. There are IT services that require couriers to transport discs around the world. There are IT services that require code to be run and monitored actively – especially the legacy code still used in the civil service and many financial institutions. But, even here, the resource available to keep the services functioning is usually greater than that actually delivering the service.

It is interesting that ITIL doesn't actually have a process for 'delivering the service'.

Summary of contents

In this investigation, we will start in Chapter 1 by looking at the change/control loops that are required to deliver and support a stable IT Service Operation system. We consider stability, adaptability and transformation loops as applied to incidents, problems and request fulfilment and find other loops and processes that are missing in ITIL. In Chapter 2 we will then look at the functions and processes for providing support in a little more detail, with a focus on the service desk role and workflows for incidents and requests including the organisational groups involved. In Chapter 3 we look at the processes involved in developing a service and how they fit together before examining the communications issues – intra-, extra- and inter-project – that can influence a project's success. In this context we also touch on Agile and DevOps. In Chapters 4 and 5, the remaining ITIL processes that manage the service and the service organisation respectively are investigated with a view to their roles in resource provision, requirements definition, reporting, coordination, innovation and governance.

In Chapter 6 we take an in-depth look at the organisational structures used in delivering IT Service Management. This is done both theoretically – to explain the approach – and by example to show how to use it. Finally, in Chapter 7, IT outsourcing is presented, some of the difficulties associated with it – and how to fix them.

Chapter 8 provides a visual summary of the book and some conclusions about the grouping of ITIL processes and applicability. We finish with further recommended reading.

Chapter 1

Supporting the Service

For many, the core of IT Service Management, and indeed ITIL, is the processes that provide direct support to keep an IT service running. In ITIL 2 these processes were in the Service Support section of ITIL, in ITIL 3 they are in the Service Operation section.

The greatest value of these processes is their clear definition of incident and problem management, and request fulfilment. Without these, there is a tendency for service desks or delivery personnel to mix them up, resulting in confusion about what is being done and how. As well as these three processes, Service Operation includes event management – a precursor to incidents, and access management – a special type of request deriving from security requirements.

Before we look at these, we need to establish the context, or framing, of this investigation.

The frame for Service Operation processes

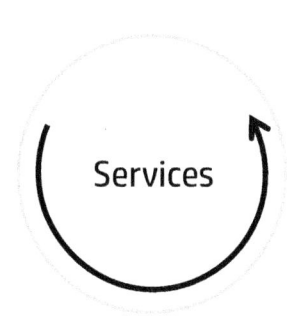

Figure 1.1 – The service delivery loop

Services are the core of any IT organisation. It is acknowledged that there are large services containing smaller services containing even smaller services – please see 'Definition of a Service' in the Introduction. We will not try here, to define exactly what a service is; the comments here are applicable regardless of the size of the service. More important is what a service does and the fact that by definition it can do it again and again. Hence, although a service can be represented by an arrow – suggesting service delivery – it is more appropriate to represent it as a looped arrow, which brings the service back to the start each time it is used. For example, once you have used an email package and closed it down, you know that, disasters excluded, it will be waiting for you to use again next time you want to send or read an email. This is the first loop we will identify and it is the delivery loop. However, we are not going to discuss this further at this time but see the start of Chapter 2 for more detail.

Control/change loops

The main frame for the Service Operation processes in support is a set of loops that are designed to maintain each service as 'fit for purpose' – see Figure 1.2. These include loops of various sizes – representing the extent and purpose of the change required to do this. These are loops because they restore the service to what is required for it to continue to function. All of these are also types of feedback loop.

Stability loops

The purpose of a **stability loop** is to maintain a service within normal operational parameters. A non-IT example often given is a house thermostat – which keeps the house temperature within a pre-set operating range. Essentially it maintains a (reasonably) stable temperature in the house. Stability loops work by measuring the output of the operational process (the service) and then comparing it with the pre-set standards – which may be temperatures, as in the example given, or other qualitative or quantitative standards depending on the service under consideration.

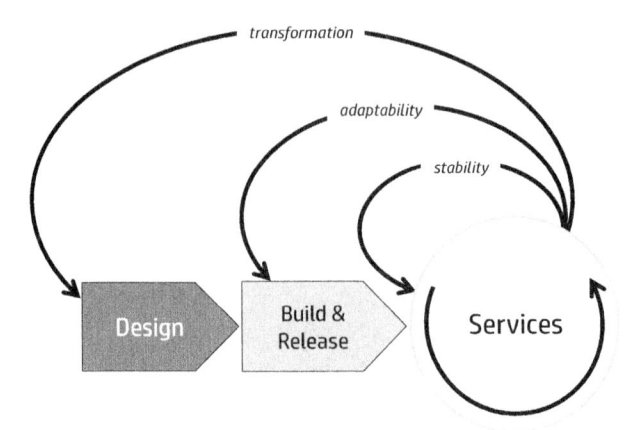

Figure 1.2 – The full set of Service Management loops

The controls available for a stability loop tend to be similarly standardised – in the example given a timer and a temperature setting – which is appropriate as the complexity is low.

Because of their (usually) simple and standard nature, stability loops don't normally need to go through design, build and release processes – even change control is normally pre-agreed. They are therefore shown as returning directly to the service in Figure 1.2 above.

Adaptability loops

The purpose of an **adaptability loop** is to modify a service so that it operates better and/or can be maintained more readily. This can be done by modifying pre-set standards – either quantitatively or qualitatively. However, it may be done by modifying the service slightly, so long as the essence of the desired function is maintained. Our non-IT example of this is to change the desired temperature on a thermostat resulting from changed usage requirements – such as people finding it too stuffy (another measurement). In this case, the change made needs conscious input and the new conditions are not predetermined until the requirement is specified.

Because of their slightly greater complexity and non-standard nature, it is normal practice for adaptability loops to require some project management to feed back into the service via build, testing and release processes, and to be under change control.

Transformation loops

The purpose of a **transformation loop** is on a considerably grander scale. There are no restrictions here on what aspects of a service may be changed and the change can be pretty fundamental – replacing one process with another and ranging from the fairly minor. e.g. replacing a mechanical thermostat with an electronic thermostat to the major, e.g. investing in full insulation.

The fundamental feature of all these transformation loops is that they require resource to implement, including planning, design and finance. Hence they require a degree of authorisation from higher management. This means that diagrammatically they are shown passing upwards through a line marked 'management level' (Figure 1.3). In reality, adaptability loops graduate into transformation loops – there is no clear delineation that provides the boundary other than a need for extra resource and approval.

Other places where control loops have been described

Similar change and control loops have been described in many other contexts: one of the best known is organisational learning. Argyris talked about single and double loop learning: His single loop learning corresponds to the adaptability loop and his double loop learning to the transformation loop. See Figure 1.3. The stability loop is not a learning loop as its role is not to learn but to provide stability.

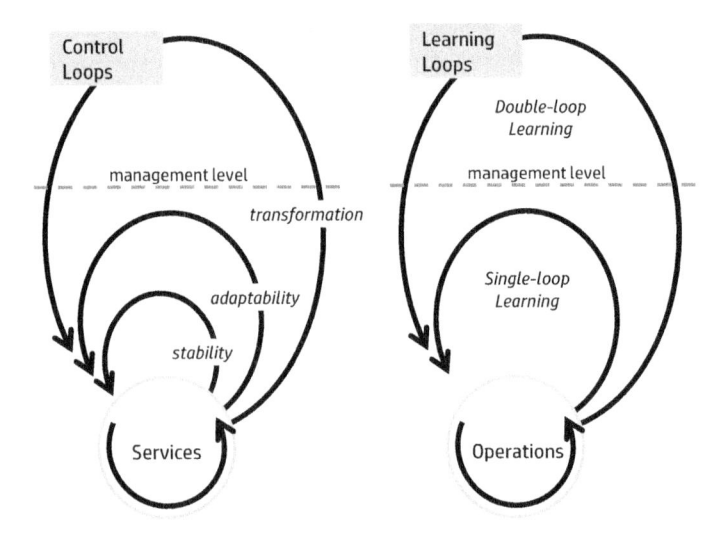

Figure 1.3 Comparions of Service Management (control) loops and learning loops.

The Kaizen and lean six sigma improvement processes are also adaptability loops which have the purpose (as always) to improve the operation of the stability loop. In the case of lean six sigma, the purpose is to reduce the frequency of 'products' or other outcomes going outside the six sigma standard.

More comprehensively and academically, Stafford Beer describes the control loops as cybernetic loops – a term which we usually misunderstand as being related to automation or robots. However, the term cybernetics comes from the Greek for 'navigator' and may be loosely translated as control.

Types of loops

There are also three fundamental types of loops, depending on who or what drives them:

- Loops which arise reactively to the detection of issues/failures in the service and which then correct them – driven by the support organisation – we will call these **troubleshooting** loops

- Loops which arise proactively from requests by the user as their requirements for a particular service shift and evolve – driven by the customer organisation – we will call these **request fulfilment** loops

- Loops which arise from proactive management of the service lifecycle as products are updated and equipment ages – driven by the supplier organisations – we will call these **service lifecycle** loops

All of these loops have the purpose of ensuring the service continues to meet the customer needs.

In the following sections, each of these three types of loop is divided into the loops of various sizes discussed above. Broadly speaking, stability loops are high-volume, low-complexity, low-value processes while the adaptability and transformation loops are small-volume, higher-complexity and higher-value processes.

Troubleshooting loops – *failure driven*

Failure-driven troubleshooting loops comprise a significant part of IT support and this is reflected by the emphasis they receive in ITIL. They include two of the named Service Operation processes – namely incident and problem management.

Troubleshooting loops are a reaction to something wrong or inadequate with the service. In Figure 1.4 these are depicted showing the loops increasing in magnitude with two different processes. This is appropriate in terms of the

Reframing ITIL

scale of change triggered, the resource needed to solve an issue and also the time needed for completion. Clearly there can be overlap, for example between a large incident requiring change control and a small problem, but broadly this is true.

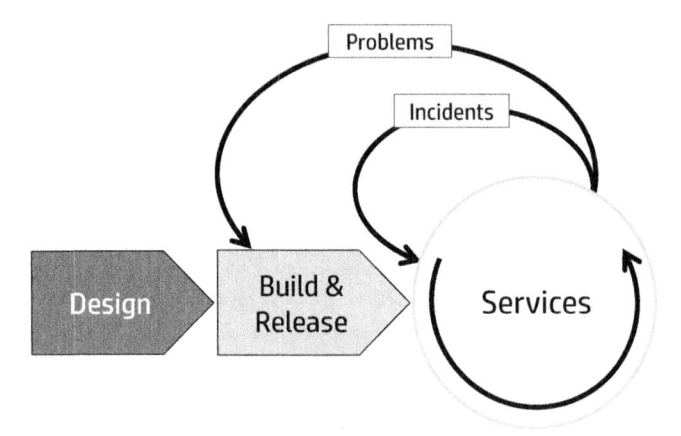

Figure 1.4. Troubleshooting service support loops in ITIL

Incident management

Incident management is an example of a classic stability loop. Incidents can arise from two inputs: those raised by users and those raised (sometimes with intervention) by events. The stability loop involves a comparison of the output of a process with expected standards (Figure 1.5); in the case of user-raised incidents, this is an implicit standard such that the user believes there is something wrong, performance is slow, the system isn't doing what is expected, perhaps it isn't working at all.

User-raised incidents

It is possible for some user-raised incidents to be 'fixed' by providing information to the user which essentially changes their expectations as in "no, it isn't actually meant to do that," or perhaps "sorry it's slow, we're doing a backup, it'll be fine in half an hour". Such incidents can even be pre-empted by providing this information in online systems which pre-empt the contact, or even, if a major incident, by emailing all users.

More usually, information can be provided which allows the user to fix the incident, as in providing instructions as to how to perform a task that has been causing problems. As we will see below, one way this is done is through 'known errors' which are identified during problem management.

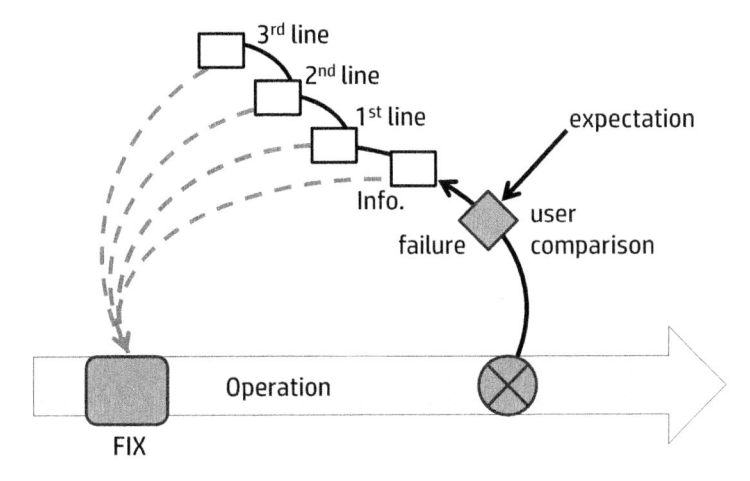

Figure 1.5 The flow of an incident

Beyond this the support personnel can often fix an incident remotely, offline or sometimes by providing 'deskside' support. This may be done through a waterfall of expertise provided by '1st line', '2nd line', '3rd line', etc. support. See Figure 1.5.

These different levels of support are offered by teams of staff with increasing levels of expertise and may also be assumed to require increasing amounts of cost and effort. This is described in more detail in the next chapter.

In all cases the main function of incident management is to fix the immediate issue and get the users working again – i.e. stability. Should any underlying issues be identified then these should be passed forward for problem management.

Automated (event-raised) incidents and major incidents
In most large IT implementation, there is control software monitoring many aspects of the hardware and software which detects 'events' – undesirable activity or behaviour. These events are then filtered – automatically and/or manually and some are identified as requiring intervention. In most implementations of ITIL-aligned monitoring software, when an event is identified as needing intervention, an incident is automatically raised.

Depending on the local rules being applied, this may include automated intervention. Regardless, the purpose of the automation of incident detection is to ensure that the potential for user disruption is avoided by fixing the incident promptly.

Automated incidents normally arise from performance/capacity/availability issues or sometimes from system failure. In the last case particularly, user disruption may be unavoidable unless the failure has occurred outside office hours.

Automated incidents can be major, (potentially) affecting a large number of users – in these cases most organisations invoke a 'major incident' process. From a systemic perspective, the major incident process is identical to the normal incident process (i.e. a stability loop), but it *operates at a higher level in the organisation*, involving more senior staff and management. It also gets a much higher priority and resource is often thrown at it.

Problem management

Problems usually arise as a result of proactive analysis of incident trends, trends in monitoring data or trends in service level statistics. The problem loop is initiated by the detection of a pattern of failures. Alternatively the incident resolution activity may have proactively passed issues forward for problem resolution. See Figure 1.6. In all cases there is a problem triage activity to select which issues should undergo problem management. The purpose of the problem management loop is to find a root cause for the problem and then fix it (if simple), recommend a resolution if not and identify a known error in the meanwhile. Problem management is a classic example of an adaptability loop.

Problem management however, often does not complete the loop to adapt the service. If the problem is not easily fixable, the outcome is a recommendation which is placed into the Continual Improvement (CI) register.

The problem-solving processes that are used in problem management are not of particular interest here, but come from the standard set of continual improvement tools including 'fish-bone diagrams', the 'five whys' and so forth. Of more interest to us systemically are the outcomes.

The first outcome arises if the problem is simple to fix with little resource. In this case, an action is taken to fix it – this is a stability loop.

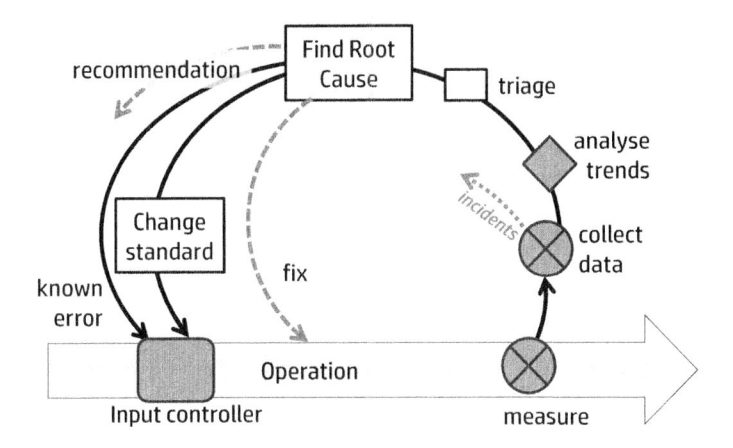

Figure 1.6. The flow of a problem

The second outcome would be along the lines of: this can be fixed by changing the standard applied to the stability loop. Hence, by altering a limit, the incident may occur far less frequently – for example, changing the performance expectation of a piece of software as capacity is reduced and the performance slows, could reduce the number of automatic incidents generated. This is an adaptability loop.

The third outcome is the generation of a 'known error'. This means that the process has resulted in understanding of the issue, but has not (yet) resolved it. The known error will be documented in an information system for the frontline support team (e.g. a service desk) so that they know how to manage incidents arising from it more effectively. It may even be documented in a user-accessed information system to pre-empt contact and in exceptional cases may be proactively communicated to users. This outcome is either the result of a realisation that the error cannot be corrected (perhaps it is the responsibility of a third party), that it is not likely to be cost-effective to correct it, or alternatively may be a holding measure while resource is organised and a corrective activity is carried out. This holding action is also an adaptability loop.

Finally, if it is decided that the problem should be resolved (the fourth outcome), then details and recommendations are placed in the Continual Improvement (CI) register for further prioritisation and consideration.

Depending on the outcome, this would likely result in completion of an adaptability or transformation loop depending on the scale of the work required.

It should be noted here that the Continual Service Improvement (CSI) process can also generate items for the CI Register – CSI uses similar problem-solving processes to problem management. From here onward their resolution is identical to the resolution of problems.

Request fulfilment loops – *user driven*

Request fulfilment loops are initiated as a result of pro-active requests from the users and client. The purpose of these loops is essentially to expand the service quantitatively of qualitatively through delivery of additional (copies of) IT software or infrastructure. See Figure 1.7.

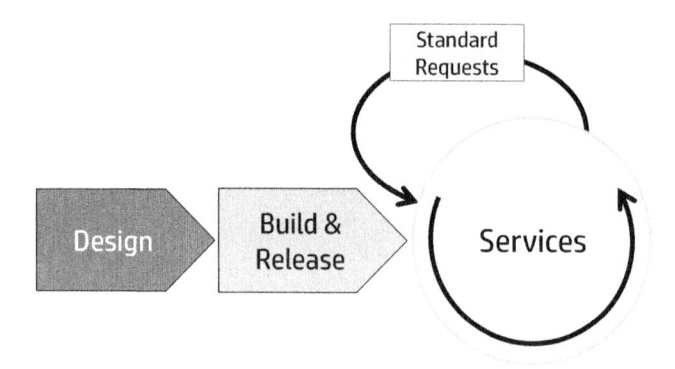

Figure 1.7 Request fulfilment service support loops in ITIL

In a larger context, request management is similar to sales or purchases as money can change hands between the client and the IT supplier. Clearly if they are both part of the same organisation this is an internal transfer and if there is a contract with an outsourcer, the payment may already have been made. In other cases, the payment may need authorisation by higher management.

Standard request fulfilment is a stability loop because, although a new instance is normally added to the service from the request fulfilment, the service itself is unchanged. Just as when you buy a copy of a piece of software such as Adobe Photoshop, the software itself is still available for another purchase.

These loops are recognised in ITIL as request fulfilment or access management. However, 'larger' loops (adaptability or transformation) are not explicitly described in ITIL and this omission can cause problems in IT Service Management (ITSM) implementation – see below.

Request fulfilment

As defined in ITIL, request fulfilment is a *standard request* process that delivers pre-defined services. This means that they are pre-costed and pre-approved – also that no change management is required for them to be delivered as the change has been pre-assessed. This, of course, does leave quite a lot out! Because of this pre-definition, it is common for requests to be ordered and delivered automatically, whether software downloads, hardware deliveries or activities such as backup or restore.

In other cases, support personnel may 'take the order' and enter it into the request processing system. Delivery may involve remote or 'deskside' support to complete installation or configuration.

Access management

As defined in ITIL, access management is also a *standard request* process that is restricted to control the access of a user to a service. The access may need to be authorised and part of the process is concerned with ensuring this – security management frequently being involved. Other parts of access management are concerned with providing access to new users or removing it from ex-users. An ongoing part of the process is password resets and refreshes. Although management and security are sometimes involved, most of this process should be managed automatically with automated process flows to ensure that the correct individuals are contacted, and the access itself is of course a process in software.

The access management loop is nearly always a minor change, with the only variant being the need to implement it for a large number of users at once which could move it to the adaptability loop category, with project and change controls required. However, generally speaking, adding new users or changing passwords does not alter the service and it stays as a stability loop.

The missing Service Operation processes

At this point we have pretty much exhausted the ITIL-defined Service Operation processes – consisting of incident (and event), problem and access management, and request fulfilment. However, in reality, there are more types of operational loops and we need to add these to give the full picture. Underemphasising or ignoring these loops is one of the causes of some of the problems in ITIL compliant IT support organisations. There is no sign that these loops have been recognised in ITIL 4.

Our first missing loop is the request fulfilment adaptability loop.

Non-standard requests

We will call the adaptability, request fulfilment loops non-standard requests (Figure 1.8). In some organisations they are *actually* called non-standard requests (NSRs), in others, significant change, complex service requests, requests for change, in others small projects – or indeed several of these names if they are scaled (see Figure 1.9).

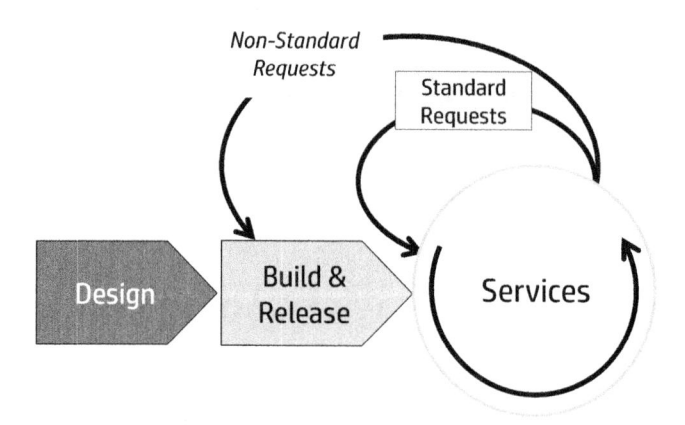

Figure 1.8 Non-standard request fulfilment loops in ITIL

Although nothing in ITIL excludes the idea of non-standard requests, there is no named process for these. The result in some organisations (and contracts), is that they are not planned for and they can be the most expensive omission in an outsourced IT environment. However, they usually rear their heads pretty assertively and often expensively!

Essentially, a non-standard request is any service or thing that a user wants that is not in the standard request catalogue and is too small to be considered a full-blown project. They always invoke the change process to a greater or lesser extent and often require some degree of project management. Examples range from the minor: a small hardware item that is non-standard – such as a monitor from a 'different' supplier, or an item that is frequently bought but that needs change management to install/implement (and hence cannot be a standard request) – to the major: such as installation of a new facility using a standard approach and an established team, or design of a new module for a piece of software. Major non-standard requests get very close to full blown projects but because the approaches are repeated, they do not usually require the involvement of the next management layer.

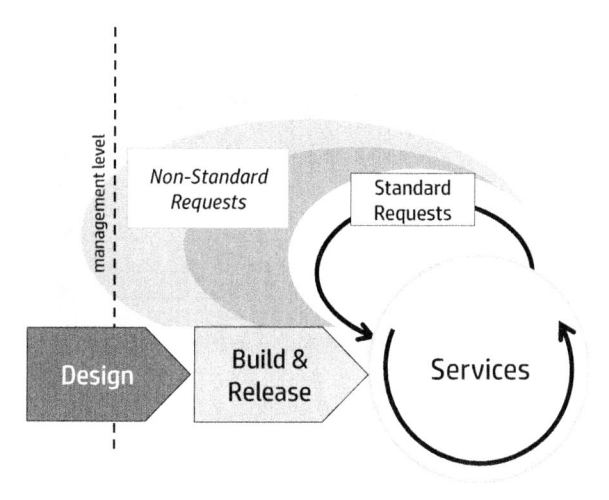

Figure 1.9 Non-standard request loops can be of various sizes

Non-standard requests represent a range of adaptability loops (Figure 1.9). They are not stability loops because the change is sufficient to leave the IT estate in a qualitatively new configuration and each have to be dealt with as one-offs. Potentially a non-standard request could result in a new type of standard request being designed and instituted if appropriate.

The scale of these loops can vary significantly – from the very small to extremely large as shown in Figure 1.9. Indeed, at the extreme some may require management approval before implementation and hence become transformation loops.

The key feature that distinguishes non-standard requests is that they cannot use the cost-effective, pre-designed and approved, standard request processes and they should not use the full-blown transformation project processes. The overhead of doing the latter would frequently exceed – sometimes many times over – the value of the request. This means that without a (range of) pre-designed non-standard request processes, there is confusion, cost-overruns and general unhappiness. Making sure that several such processes are prepared and implemented is therefore key to cost-effective delivery of request fulfilment.

Service lifecycle management loops – *supplier driven*

There is also a whole set of Service Operation loops missing in a third type of loop – supplier-driven change: Service lifecycle management loops are recognised in ITIL but are not explicitly described as processes.

Service lifecycle management loops renew, or can even replace, the service: This third set of control loops are found in the 'service lifecycle' arena where loops are proactively initiated as a result of changes to the available technology from the technology suppliers – i.e. they are principally 'supplier driven' and are all proactive. The purpose of these loops is essentially to maintain and renew the technology available to the users. See Figure 1.10.

Although these loops are entirely logical and necessary, because they are not emphasised in ITIL, in poorly planned support organisations one or both may be missing or under-resourced. The stability and adaptability loops are as follows.

Chapter 1 – Supporting the Service

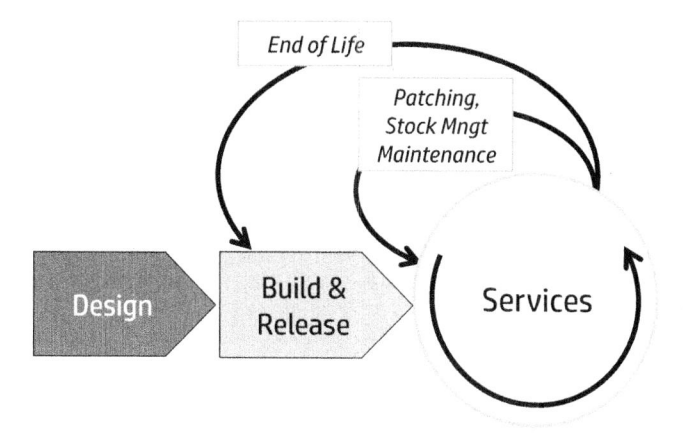

Figure 1.10 Supplier driven service support loops

Patching and stock management

Both patching and stock management processes are examples of stability loops. Both processes are pro-actively initiated by the support organisation.

Patching to software is usually carried out following the receipt of patches from a third-party supplier. At this point, the configuration of the IT system needs to be 'patched' to bring it back to the current standard. In most large-scale service organisations, this is managed and controlled by the IT support organisation who will check that patches will not disrupt the system and that there are no security risks. They may also bundle patches together to reduce disruption and cost. In smaller support organisations and for COTS (commercial, off the shelf) products, patching may be automated using the update system supplied – e.g. by Microsoft or Adobe.

Stock management at this stability level is about ensuring that there are sufficient items of stock available to meet the needs of standard requests. This is normally done by refreshing the stock when levels drop to or below a critical level. An alternative would be to 'outsource' this activity to the stock supplier so that the stock is ordered directly and none is kept in store. Again, the former is more likely to be done in a larger organisation and the latter in a smaller organisation. Whoever does this, the purpose is to restore the stock level to the set level.

Maintenance

Maintenance is also pro-active and the prompt or initiator for it is normally a schedule. As the purpose of maintenance is to keep the service operating as planned, it clearly represents a stability loop. Although maintenance can come in small, medium and even large chunks – often requiring 'service or system downtime', all of these are really scaled stability loops. It would not be accurate to describe any of these as high volume.

End-of-life – refresh

End-of-life management is a refresh of IT service components and is a classic example of an adaptability loop. As with most of the service lifecycle loops, it is initiated by suppliers and occurs when a major software upgrade, or a new model of a hardware item is released. Examples of this would be an upgrade from MS Office to the next version or from one 'standard laptop' to a new model. End of life modifies the operational system by replacing components with new ones across the board (eventually).

For these upgrades to occur, the new software or hardware need to be tested to ensure that they still meet all the system requirements – including in particular security and integration with other components of the IT service. Then the new items will be allowed into the request catalogue for new users and an upgrade cycle may be started. Alternatively and for hardware in particular, a decision may be taken to replace old models only as they reach a specified, age.

In the absence of an end-of-life process, these upgrades are treated as 'one offs', or mini-projects. This introduces the same over-cost issues as non-standard requests above.

Transformation loops

Transformation loops are a little different from the stability and adaptability loops discussed up to now, in that they occur not solely within the Service Operation context, but pass outside and upwards into the organisation (see next chapter).

As they include the whole ITSM lifecycle, it is perhaps not surprising that they do not have named processes. Nonetheless, recognising them in the contexts of the three types does provide clarity for their roles (Figure 1.11).

Transformations may be initiated by a contract, or be driven by an improvement programme, user requests or lifecycle renewal and encompass both of the major delivery processes – infrastructure and applications: Sometimes improvement projects can be dealt with at the adaptability loop level. However, what usually elevates this activity to a transformation loop is the need for design and significant resource to fix an issue. Service Design and Service Transition processes are invoked, as is project management. All require significant resource and require management commitment at a higher level. This may involve a reallocation of existing resource or use of new resource.

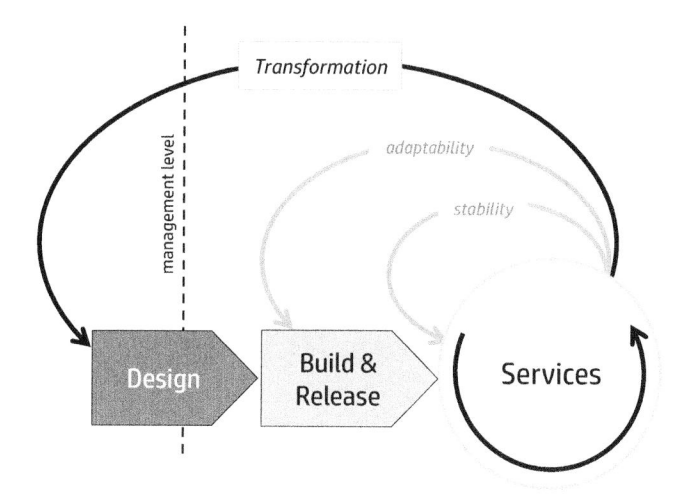

Figure 1.11 Transformation service management loops

In most cases, transformation projects are planned and remedial rather than truly innovative.

Improvement projects

Improvement projects are not a process found in Service Operation – rather they represent one of the types of project requiring the full ITSM Lifecycle. Issues surfaced by problem management or Continual Service Improvement are logged in the Continual Improvement register and then form the basis of discussions between the ITSM management and the (client) business. These discussions prioritise which projects will go forward.

Transformation requests
Most transformation requests come through at senior level from the business organisation to the IT department (or IT outsourcer, if there is one). Some may even be defined in a contract in the latter case. Transformation requests are fulfilled through classic transformation loops – they represent another of the types of project requiring the full ITSM lifecycle. What distinguishes this loop from the smaller request loops is the need for significant resource to fulfil them

Renewal programmes
Renewal programmes describe a transformation of one or more of the IT service components and are fulfilled through classic transformation loops. The renewal is initiated originally by a change in technology – often by a third-party supplier, sometimes by the IT service provider. Most renewal programmes are agreed at a senior level between the business organisation, the IT department (and, if involved, the IT outsourcer). Some may even be built into contracts in the last case.

Examples would be the virtualisation of servers, moving file storage into the cloud, or moving from desktop to handheld products; essentially any major, step change with significant implications.

Summary

The main operational support processes in ITIL are all feedback loops, demonstrating the three basic types: stability, adaptability and transformation loops. Incident, problem, request fulfilment and access management (standard requests) are all processes in Service Operation. Continual Service Improvement, although portrayed as one of the major processes, is closely akin to problem management. These loops have the characteristics shown in Table 1.1 and Figure 1.12 below.

Only incident management (encompassing also event management), problem management and request fulfilment (including access management) are emphasised as full processes in ITIL. However, if only these are implemented, absence of the missing processes may (and frequently does) cause severe difficulties when they are required during normal operation.

The 'missing' processes include the various sizes and types of non-standard request and (supplier driven) lifecycle renewal. It is not uncommon for

Chapter 1 – Supporting the Service

organisations new to service support, who are introducing ITIL, to miss these processes – storing up problems for the future.

Loop Type	Characteristics	Troubleshoot/ Operational Control	Request Fulfilment	Service Lifecycle Management
		Failure Driven	**User Driven**	**Supplier Driven**
Stability	high volume, low value, quick	Incidents	Standard Requests/ Access Mngt	Patching & Stock Mngt
Adaptability	medium volume, medium value, medium timescale	Problems	Non-Standard Requests	End-of-life, Refresh
Transformation	low volume, high value, long timescale	Problems	Transformation Requests	Renewal Programmes

Table 1.1   Characteristics of the Service Management process loops

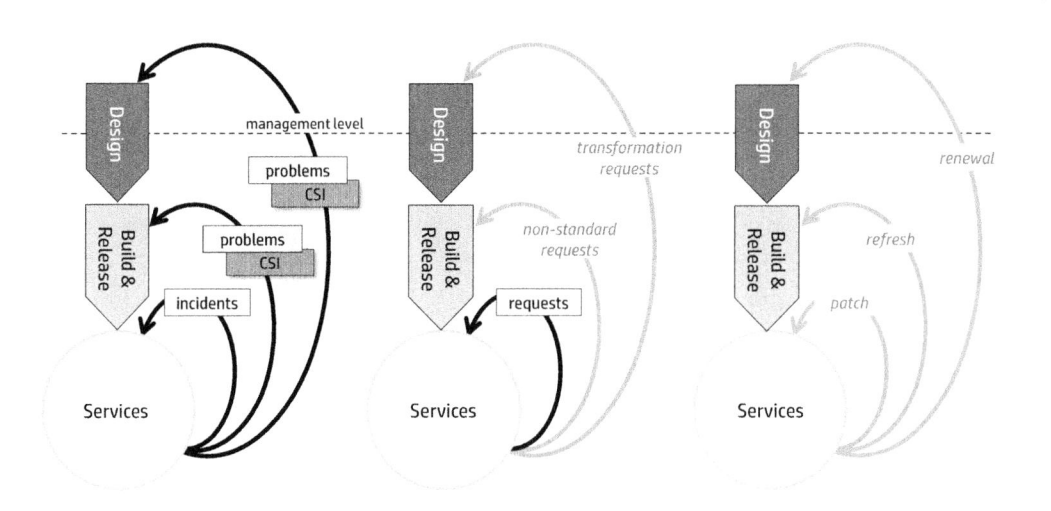

Figure 1.12   The Service Management process loops

19

Delivering the service

The last, and in many cases, least activity that support staff engage in is the delivery of the service itself. The term itself can be confusing – particularly in ITIL where Service Delivery described a whole set of 'service management' processes in ITIL 2. However, here we use it to mean the service, itself, as it is being used.

Because of the nature of IT, most of the services are automatic and 'deliver themselves' – with a bit of help from the user who is using them. For example, an email service is entirely automatic – no one takes your email and delivers it actively to the recipient. This is in contrast to paper mail which involves numerous personal interventions to delivery – from the mail van drivers through the sorting office staff to the lorry or train drivers and the postman or woman.

Figure 1.13 – The Service delivery Loop

One exception, which is not completely automated, as mentioned above, is the backup and restore service which has a dedicated team in many organisations – although this too is now frequently automated. Other examples of support staff engaging in actual service delivery include running batch computer programs – usually using legacy technologies such as are frequently found in the financial sector and central government. Some services that are still manually operated are those at the periphery of IT such as delivering bills or cheque payments – these are prepared automatically and then printed on high-capacity printers and dispatched manually. Again, newer technologies make all these processes automatic and electronic.

It should be noted that in areas other than IT, the delivery of the service can represent the biggest draw on resource – medical support or the railways being good examples.

What works and what doesn't work?

The main advantage of following the ITIL Service Operation processes is that they clearly separate out a number of functions – incident and problem management and request fulfilment – that can otherwise get mixed up and confused.

Incidents and problems

In particular, in an organisation without ITIL, service support staff can get involved in investigating and fixing an interesting problem arising from an incident (the two may be confused in the minds of the support staff). Although this can help the user raising the incident, everyone else has to wait and this causes dissatisfaction. Keeping the two processes separate means that fixing incidents becomes a priority, thus keeping users as happy as possible. The problem still gets looked at, and hopefully fixed, over a more extended time period while the users are back at work.

Requests

Request fulfilment is also frequently met through the same service desk (contact centre) where incidents are reported. This is not of itself a problem unless the service desk is under-resourced. However, standard requests can readily be automated, taking pressure off the service desk and reducing costs.

Metrics

A further advantage of having defined processes is that metrics are relatively easy to record – both the numbers of each type of incident or request and the times taken to fulfil them. This information informs management who can see where to improve matters and better ensure that the quality of service is maintained.

Bypassing newly-introduced processes

There is a common issue in organisations adopting ITIL and service desks for the first time: This is the tendency of users who know and like the old, more personal process of directly contacting support staff to carry on doing so. So long as the support staff respond to this, they can undermine the metrics and resource allocation that the new processes make possible.

The only way to fix this – other than exhortation, which rarely works – is to ensure that resource is only allocated on the basis of the visible, and new, support processes. In this way the support staff is incentivised to say no to informal approaches. An alternative way is to allow the support staff to record incidents fixed from informal, personal contacts and make them official.

Although this has some advantages, it also has disadvantages in terms of discouraging the use of the service desk.

Loops working together

The point that the loops do not work in isolation but together has already been made. However, one point has been missed so far: if the transformation and adaptability loops are done well then the stability loops are needed less. This is not necessarily true for all loop types, but is for the ones detailed below.

To take some simple examples: a really well designed piece of software (e.g. automatic bill payment) will not produce problems and will not produce many incidents. So, an effective, appropriately focused, problem management process that improves the design of such software over time will reduce the number of incidents.

The same inference can be taken for request management – if the standard requests have been carefully chosen to meet the needs of users, then the need for non-standard requests is much reduced. If all the services in standard requests are useless, then most requests will come through the non-standard route.

This is obvious, but astonishingly not how it normally works. Many IT departments have most resource focused on incident management for poorly designed and implemented services. Many IT departments have a weak or almost non-existent problem management process.

Some IT outsourcing contracts actually define payment by the number of incidents fixed. This actually encourages the continuation of large numbers of incidents and discourages setting up an effective problem management process.

Planning how the three sizes of loops (or more in the case of requests) work together is important to ensure minimum cost and disruption to services.

Chapter 2

Organising to Support the Service

The activities of a service organisation

It is probably accurate to say that a typical service organisation has three significant groups of activities: development, delivery and support.

Referring back to the loops of the previous chapter, delivery encompasses the service delivery loop (!); support encompasses the stability and adaptability loops and development combines the Service Design and Service Transition arrows (Figure 2.1).

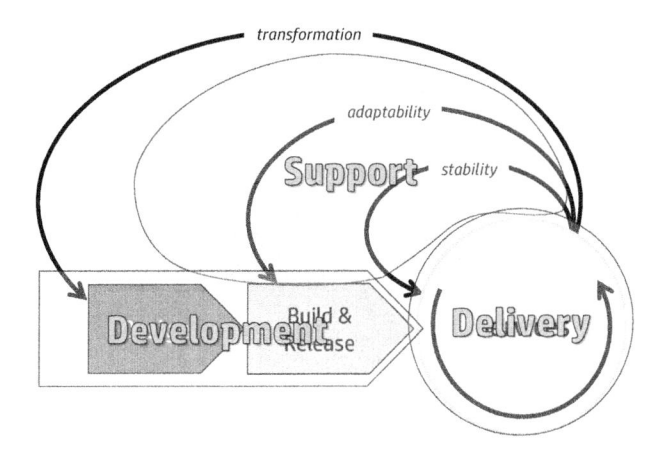

Figure 2.1 Development, delivery and support mapped onto service management loops

Development is about creating new operational services or significantly modifying existing ones. Delivery is about the ongoing delivery of the services

Reframing ITIL

to the user or to an intermediate service. Support is about ensuring that the operational services work and are appropriate for a specific user.

We can place these three sets of activities into three operational groups:

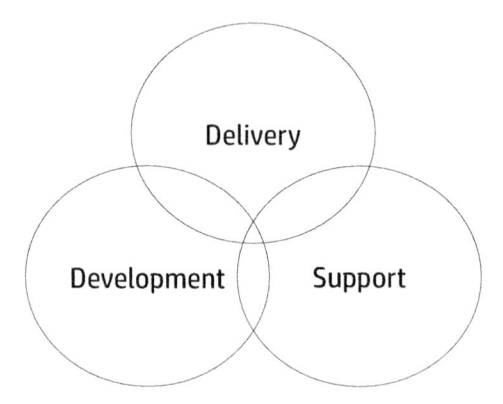

Figure 2.2 The activities of Service Management

In Figure 2.2 they are shown as overlapping because the activities that each of them perform frequently do overlap.

The important point for this investigation is that we are going to dispense with the delivery activity in our further discussion of the IT organisation. This is not because delivery is not important, clearly it is critical, but because in IT it is almost entirely automated – that is after all, one of the main purposes of IT.

If we were discussing the railways, or the health service, then delivery could represent the largest operational activity but, in IT, it is minor. We are therefore going to assume that the residual IT delivery activities such as 'backup and restore', or running batch jobs for legacy applications, are carried out in support. So, in future organisational models/diagrams, only development and support will be shown since these are dealing with groups of activities and processes carried out by people.

ITIL 2

Those readers familiar with ITIL 2 will be used to a completely different use of these terminologies which groups ITIL processes in completely different ways but does use both the terms Service Delivery (for various management processes) and Service Support (for a mixture of support and development processes). Please bear with us over the next chapters as we reframe this.

Chapter 2 – Organising to Support the Service

We will call the whole set of delivery and support activities service operations – this is not the same as ITIL's use of the term Service Operation which is capitalised throughout.

A simple organisational model

Taking the above point on board, and having looked at the operational loops involved in supporting and delivering a service, it is now worth looking in more detail into who performs these activities and where they might sit in the organisation. To do this we need to introduce an organisational model which we will then build on throughout later chapters of this book.

The basic model is indeed very basic, as shown in Figure 2.3 – with two components – management and operations. Despite its simplicity, its main trick is that it is applicable at any level in the organisation. So this could be used to describe the whole business, the IT department, a technical team and so forth – this gives what is known as a recursive structure.

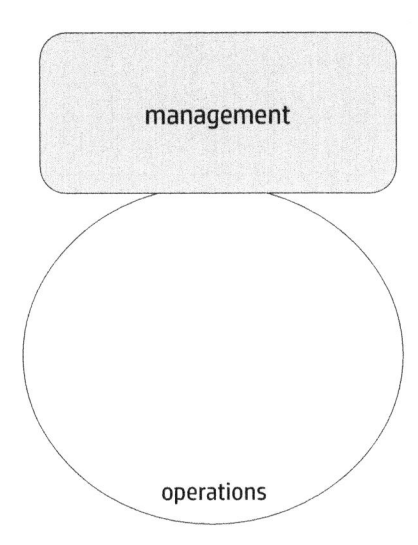

Figure 2.3 A simple organisational model for a single layer of the organisation

Using this recursive principle, if we want to look at two levels in the organisation, we can depict them as shown in Figure 2.4.

This illustrates that each level of the organisation is nested within the operations group of the level above it. If there is more than one group in a level (and there always is – except at the very top level), then both or more are found together in the operations group. In the example shown, there are two groups.

To make this more specific to IT and ITIL, if the higher level of this simple organisation is the service, then the two lower levels could be development and support – between them making up service operations.

Reframing ITIL

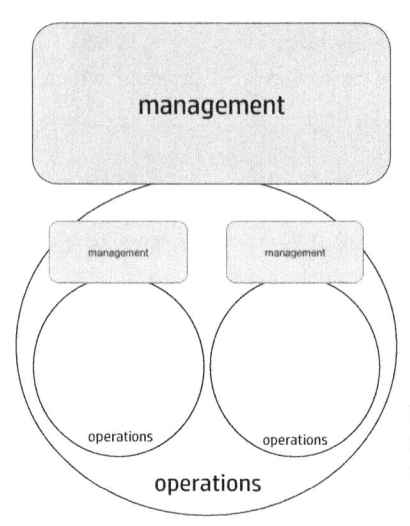

Using this organisational model enables us to see where loops, processes and other activities may take place. We can then build it up as required to examine different aspects of the interrelationships between these and the organisations they sit in.

Figure 2.4 A simple organisational model showing two levels of the organisation

Fitting Service Management loops into the organisation

Referring back to the stability, adaptability and transformation control loops introduced in the previous chapter, when identified as ITIL processes they fit broadly into the organisation as shown in Figure 2.5. Note that the operations activities in development are projects and the operations activities in support are mainly technical support – including, where appropriate, technical or service resolver groups.

The stability loops can normally be completed entirely by operations in the support group. Also very few fixes or

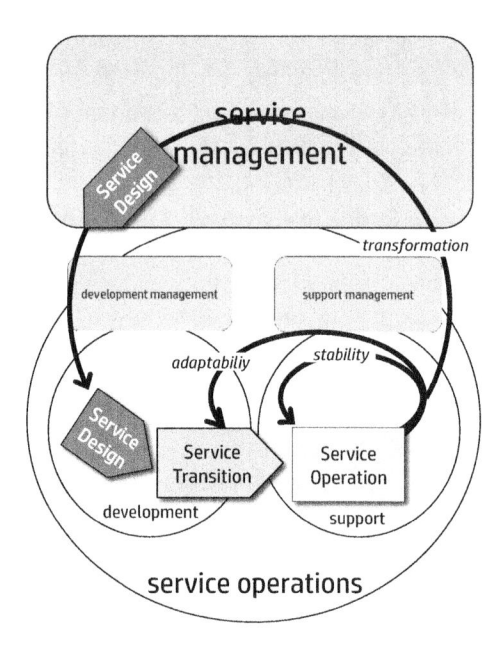

Figure 2.5 Mapping the service management loops onto the bi-level organisational model

26

standard requests require development resource.

In some organisations, the adaptability loops are also carried out in support, but it is more common for these larger fixes or non-standard requests to seek some input from operations technical teams in the development group (but usually without significant management input). In some situations adaptability activities may be run as small projects – without significant design input – in which case they feed into the Service Transition processes as shown.

The large transformation loops, by contrast, do require management input from the service level above because they need to be prioritised and resources need to be allocated for their completion. Design input (high level design) is also required at this level to ensure that the design is consistent with standards and that other parts of the service are not adversely impacted. Once a project is set up and running, further design input (low level design) is carried out in development operations. Normally, all design input is made by the service architects who are able (like some others) to work at whichever organisational level they are required to.

Focusing on stability loops in the support group

In the previous chapter we started to look at the 'small but frequent' stability loops identified as the ITIL processes of incident management, request fulfilment and access management. In incident management we also introduced the idea that incidents may be managed sequentially by a waterfall of expertise. At this point we are going to look at the structures, issues and processes that fit here in a little more detail. We can reasonably assume that the 'stability' loops, resulting from users contacting the IT group about an incident or a request, will take place in the support group.

However, this does not just happen. Somehow the user needs to contact the right support group to carry out their request or resolve their incident. In principle, this can be done directly but, for that to work, the user would need to know which support group to contact.

If there were one support group for each service, as it is understood by a user, then this would be relatively straightforward. However, it is very rare for support organisations to be structured like this.

Reframing ITIL

ITIL typically identifies technology groups to perform fixes and fulfil requests. It locates the technology support groups in a department called IT Operations and then groups them into applications and infrastructure operations.

This can look something like the following once the infrastructure operations are broken out into sub-types:

- Applications
- Network Infrastructure
- Telecommunications
- Server Infrastructure
- Desktop

Each of these can be broken down into lower level technologies as in this example:

- Applications
    - Application A – e.g. a business support system
    - Application B – e.g. an HR system
    - Application C – e.g. a payment system
- Network Infrastructure
    - LAN (local area network)
    - WAN (wide area network)
    - Internet/Web
- Telecommunications
    - Mobile
    - Fixed link
- Server Infrastructure
    - Cloud
    - Unix
    - Windows
- Desktop
    - PC/laptop/tablet etc..
    - Operating System
    - Desktop Applications
    - Email

Depending on the nature of the IT organisation, applications may include dozens of technologies and bespoke applications which require the vast majority of technology support. Alternatively an IT organisation may be

Chapter 2 – Organising to Support the Service

infrastructure only. There are also many other ways to group these activities. Essentially, though, many of these support groups will mean little to a user who would be totally confused if faced with a list like this when trying to work out who to contact.

If we take a typical service such as in-house email, then it is fairly easy to see that it makes use of an email server, LAN and WAN networks and an email application as well as an internet gateway. It runs, for the user, on an operating system on a desktop or laptop computer or other mobile device. The emails are backed up and there may also be other, hidden, systems and applications impinging on it. This is especially the case if the emails either contain rich multimedia content, or interface with a business support system of some kind, e.g. a customer portal.

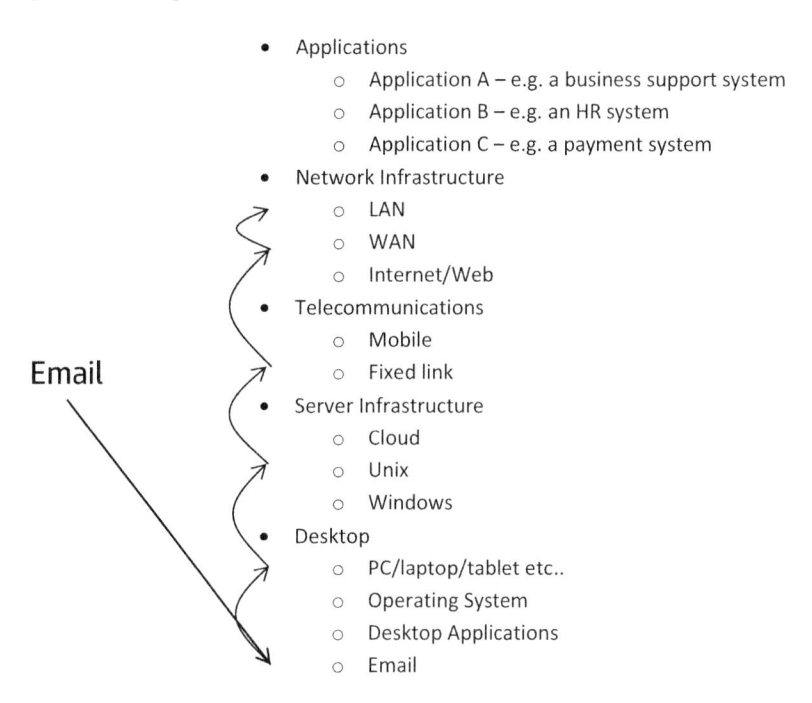

Email

- Applications
    - Application A – e.g. a business support system
    - Application B – e.g. an HR system
    - Application C – e.g. a payment system
- Network Infrastructure
    - LAN
    - WAN
    - Internet/Web
- Telecommunications
    - Mobile
    - Fixed link
- Server Infrastructure
    - Cloud
    - Unix
    - Windows
- Desktop
    - PC/laptop/tablet etc..
    - Operating System
    - Desktop Applications
    - Email

The diagram above shows an email incident being passed first to one technology group, then to another and so forth until the failure is eventually found to be in the LAN. Each of these technology groups is involved in supporting email, so this is perfectly reasonable – however, the complexity of email is greater than the end-user can sensibly be expected to understand.

Reframing ITIL

Other services may not be as complicated as email, but will have similar issues. This clearly demonstrates that there is no one-to-one relationship between a service, as used by a user, and the technical operations and organisation that support it.

So, when a service such as email goes wrong and a user wants to log an incident, it is not necessarily clear which part of the organisation needs to investigate. The user cannot tell because very likely all they know is that (for example) they are not receiving any emails.

The service desk

In order to help resolve this issue and to provide a single point of contact for the end user, most service groups make use of service desks:

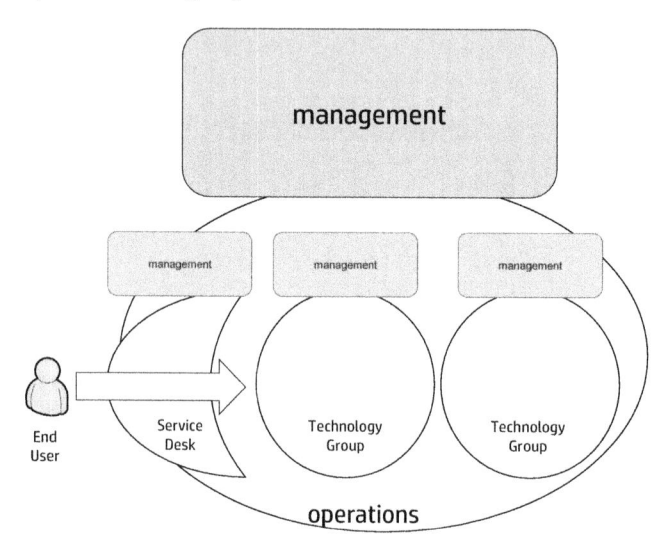

Figure 2.6 The service desk on the boundary of an operations group

Note that the service desk carries out a function on the boundary of the service operations group (although inside it) providing an interface with the end user. This is the first type of service desk – 'catch and despatch'! To illustrate this boundary role it has been given a 'half moon' shaped operations group in Figure 2.6.

Triage

When a complaint or request is raised by a user or an automated system, its first port of call on the way into the service management organisation is usually the service desk – also known as a call centre, help desk, contact centre or similar. ITIL talks of this as a function rather than a process. The key is what this service desk actually does and its main role is that of **triage**. Triage is basically deciding what to do with a call, logging it, identifying its priority and finally where to send it. The term is most commonly used in medical services but is appropriate for any service.

It is not terribly relevant what technology is used for initially contacting the service management organisation but most contact is via the telephone and increasingly this is also supported by web interfaces which may include online chat to 'talk' to a call handler. The main advantage of a web interface is that it is easy to make information directly available to the user – through announcements or through FAQs (frequently asked questions). The benefit is that this reduces the number of calls and the number of call handlers required, reducing costs. As this information is also needed by the call handlers, there is no (perhaps a little?) extra work in keeping this up to date.

What to do with a call

In fact, the three components of triage can be separated and sometimes they are: The first component of triage is **what to do with it**: Is the contact a request for information? Is it a request for a widget or service? Is it a request for a password reset? Is it a complaint about something malfunctioning? These four examples go into four separate processes: information provision, request fulfilment, access management or incident management – the latter three being ITIL processes in Service Operation. In many organisations these four requirements are separated before a call is made: information provision is accessed through a web portal; request fulfilment is accessed through an online catalogue; access management is accessed through an online password renewal system and only complaints are made to a service desk. The service desk would frequently also spend some time directing miscalls to the other appropriate mechanisms for solution!

Identifying calls correctly is important for measurements and identifying resource needs. Misidentifying non-standard requests as complaints is a way to get them into the system and get a caller off the operative's hands, but can be expensive and it is a 'back-door' way of fulfilling them. It can also hide a real need that isn't being met by the official systems. Unfortunately, some measuring systems count this to the operators' favour by managing to always reduce the call handling time. Now on to the second component of triage.

Prioritising a call

Once a complaint has been identified the call handler needs to **log it** – frequently directly as an incident – and **identify its priority**. This is where the importance of the call handling workflow system is paramount. In some cases, the system is directly linked to the call handling system and automatically monitors the call duration, with additional information being required and added by the call handler.

Priority can come in two forms – the importance of the caller (user) and the importance of the complaint/issue. In the former case, the normal distinction is between normal users and VIP users – who are often a small sub-set of users identified in a contract and including senior managers and time-critical users (such as financial stock traders). VIP users may have their own resolver teams, their own metrics and even their own contact number(s) so that the call handlers know immediately who they are dealing with. Some procedures may also be distinct for such users – such as to replace a faulty laptop rather than repair it.

Assessing the importance of a complaint, requires more judgement by the call handler, and hence more knowledge. Essentially, a judgement is made as to the importance of an incident and, if required, the incident is passed to a priority incident team. This team have access to more resources and follow a modified process that involves escalation to include more senior staff of both the client and the outsource supplier. This occurs normally when an incident has the potential to, or actually is, causing a major disruption.

Where to send a call

The third and final component of triage is **where to send it**: For this, the call handler needs to know where to send each type of query and then to do so. This is not always as easy as it sounds (see the email example above): If some level of interpretation of the query is required – perhaps the user's understanding of what they require is different from the way the organisation structures its support – then a higher level of expertise is required by the service desk operative. This also applies if the service desk operative needs to prioritise it.

A need for some interpretation is the normal situation and produces a contradiction which is that, for effective triage, a substantial level of knowledge is required but the job remains a repetitive and low-paid one. The result is even higher turnover and, a more immediate problem for the organisation, a substantial amount of misdirection of incidents and queries to the wrong expertise group – quite frequently in excess of 50%. Call misdirection not only frustrates the user/caller if they are directly involved, but also wastes time and money in the service desk and in the expertise groups.

First contact resolution

Increasingly, in many cases service desks also carry out the next step – resolution. Where this is done, only the first of the three triage stages is performed. Only after a failure to resolve the issue are prioritising a call and where to send it, invoked. The exception to this is for high priority end users, where the call may be prioritised first – often through use of a slightly different contact route – perhaps a priority phone number.

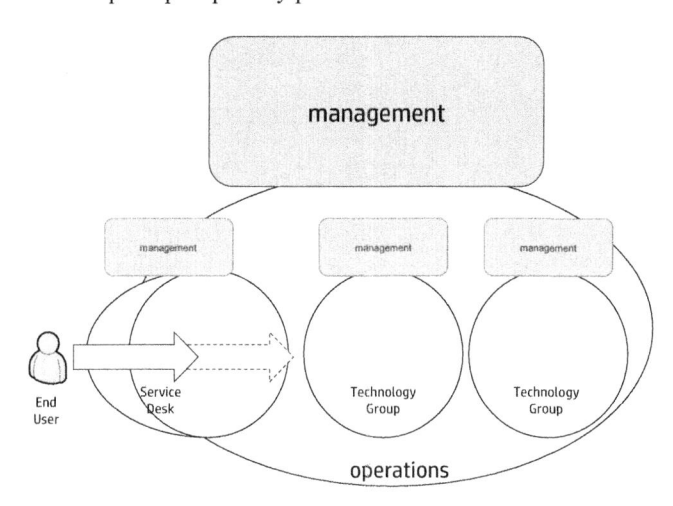

Figure 2.7 The service desk also providing resolution
in an operational group

As well as providing a simpler process for fixing simple incidents, the biggest advantage of this is that the opportunity for misallocation to technology groups is much reduced.

Although the service desk still carries out a function on the boundary of the operations group to provide an interface with the end user, it also has a role as a sort of technology group to provide first-contact resolution. This is the second type of service desk.

To provide first-contact resolution to anything like a significant proportion of incidents – 60% is often the performance target – the call handlers now need to have significant knowledge and experience, although how much does depend on the profile of the incidents raised.

In fact, although this requires staff with more experience, the reduction in the possibilities of misallocation of incidents may actually make it cost effective. To get more experienced staff, higher reward is necessary to reduce turnover – but the more interesting work also helps. However, in many situations the job remains a repetitive and low-paid one. The result is again high turnover and a continuous struggle to achieve the performance target for first-contact resolution.

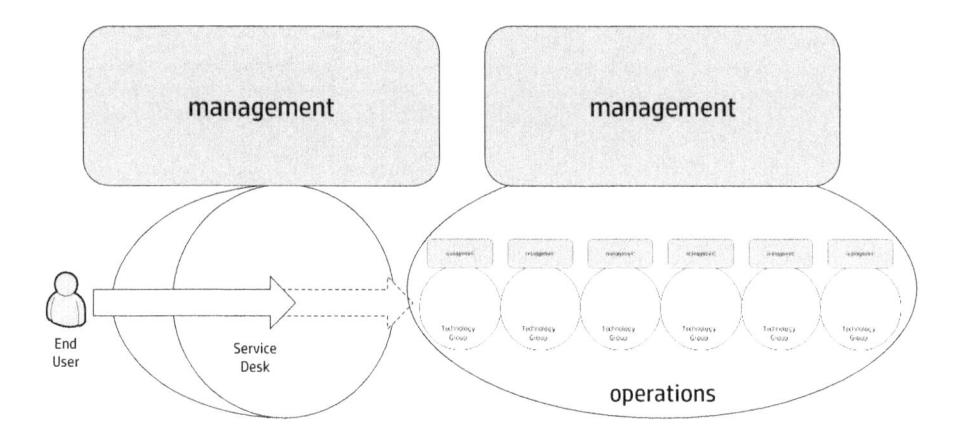

Figure 2.8 The service desk in its own part of the organisation

Most organisations ensure that there are comprehensive and valuable 'knowledge bases' available that help the call handlers find the solution to common incidents. In multi-supplier environments there can be issues of confidentiality regarding intellectual capital for the content in these systems. i.e. the service desk may need to know how to fix issues 'owned' by a range of IT suppliers.

The knowledge bases are usually the main means by which the technology groups transfer their knowledge to the service desk staff. Without a technology background, the service desk staff can struggle with anything but the simplest incidents

Chapter 2 – Organising to Support the Service

In practice, the sizes of the groups are not as represented in the simplified diagram shown in Figure 2.7, but more like those shown in Figure 2.8. Here we can see that although (for a large organisation) each of the technology groups may hold half a dozen or so staff, the service desk may hold a hundred or more. This is appropriate if the service desk is expected to resolve such a large proportion, such as 60%, of the incoming incidents.

Additionally, Figure 2.8 shows the service desk and the technology groups in different parts of the IT organisation, which they frequently are. Indeed, in more complex environments the technology groups may sit in several different departments (applications and infrastructure is an obvious example) which may be part of the support or development departments, or even different outsourced businesses.

In certain cases, a service may become inherently problematic and generate a disproportionate amount of incidents. In this case it can be worth setting up a dedicated team for the duration of the high level of incidents – which may last years.

A typical incident workflow (stability loop)

At this point, it is well worth spending some time investigating the resources that fulfil and deliver the operational processes just described. These are also well described in the ITIL Service Operation book which we recommend consulting.

Using this particular frame highlights the similarities between the organisational needs and the varieties of service support processes. This can help to show anomalies, inconsistencies and gaps in adopted processes and suggest standardisation that could improve them.

The focus will be on the stability and adaptability loops and we start with incident management – see Figure 2.9. The end-to-end incident resolution process requires input from two types of resource: these are the service desk and the technology groups – here termed resolver groups as their function is to resolve incidents.

Resolver groups are identified by ITIL as IT Operations and include infrastructure and application operations, although usually these are subdivided further in many support organisations. The incident resolution process may look something like Figure 2.9 – as a flow diagram:

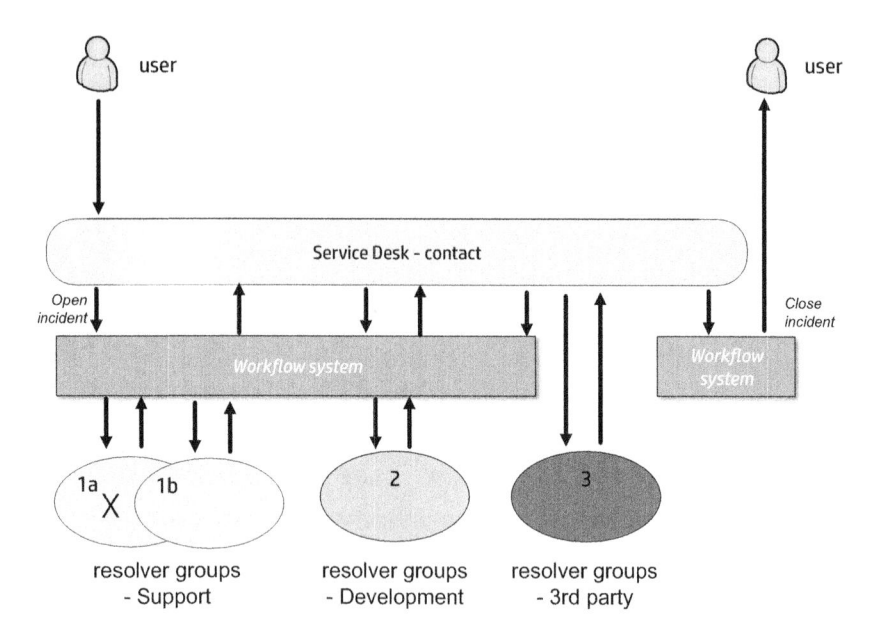

Figure 2.9 Flow diagram showing typical resource use in incident management

The convention used shows the resource pools with rounded edges and the IT system with square edges.

The flow shown is for a complicated failure that is first submitted to the service desk where it is opened as an incident in the workflow system, allocated to resolver group 1a. However, when a member of this resolver group looks at it they realise it has been misallocated and change the allocation to resolver group 1b (1 here refers to first line). 1b look at the incident and realise that it is too complicated for them to resolve and so indicate this accordingly in the workflow system which returns it to the service desk for further allocation. The service desk then allocates it to a second line resolver group (2) who are part of the development team. They also are unable to resolve the incident and also indicate this in the workflow system which again returns it to the service desk for further allocation. This time the incident needs to be looked at by a third party – who is the third line resolver group in this system. However, the third party does not have access to the workflow system and so the service desk record that they are sending this to the third party and contact them directly. The third party resolves the incident and notifies the service desk who then

Chapter 2 – Organising to Support the Service

complete the incident record and close the incident. The workflow system automatically notifies the user that the incident has been resolved.

There are clearly many possible alternatives to this workflow, including:

1. The service desk may need to intervene after the misallocation to a resolver group.
2. The service desk may NOT need to intervene before the second line resolver group are allocated the incident.
3. The third party may have access to the workflow system.
4. The service desk may NOT need to intervene before the third line resolver group are allocated the incident.
5. The service desk may need to consult with management to authorise an allocation to a third party.
6. The workflow system may notify the service desk that the incident has been resolved and they contact the user.

..and so forth.

None of these alternatives make any significant difference to the workflow, which is essentially about sending the incident to groups with increasing levels of understanding (and typically cost). However, depicting the actual workflow in this way does make it clear what is being done and identifies opportunities for improvement and/or standardisation.

One would reasonably expect that on average, most incidents are fixed by a first line group, less by a second line group and only exceptionally few by a third line group (who *may* be a third party).

Note that in this scenario, there is no first contact resolution since the service desk is carrying out a "catch and dispatch" role. As mentioned above, one of the biggest problem areas here is the high probability of initial misallocation.

In some (usually large) IT support organisations, some of the resolver groups may have their own triage function in the form of an incident coordinator who allocates incidents to particular staff.

Further possibilities to enhance incident resolution

In these scenarios, the problem of call misdirection is resolved only by the expertise of the service desk staff. There are several alternatives that can also help reduce this. These include:

- The technical staff in resolver groups may see a list of all the incidents entered into a workflow system and self-select those which are appropriate for their team. This can usually only work in small or medium sized operations.
- In particular cases – such as the email service example given above – a virtual resolver group may be made up of staff from the various technical teams likely to be involved. This could be a temporary allocation of staff to a co-located team, or could be a team constituted only virtually – using the workflow system and telecommunications to function. This allows a complicated incident to be passed between staff with different technical expertise more rapidly.

Serious incidents

Serious incidents are normally defined as incidents that might significantly impact the business of the IT client. If there is a contractual arrangement between an outsourced IT department and the business, then the conditions would be in the contract.

To manage serious incidents, most IT departments would have a separate serious incident process and, frequently, a serious incident manager distinct from the incident manager. This role might be 'part time' and additional to another role for the individual concerned.

Serious incidents frequently come into the service desk initially as normal incidents. At some point during resolution, the service desk or a technology team identify that the impact is significant and escalate the incident to the serious incident manager and the serious incident process is then invoked. In most cases this does two things: It raises the incident priority to top, bringing in additional technology resource, and it informs senior management both in IT and the client business. An incident 'call' is frequently set up which all interested parties can dial into. The resource dedicated to resolving the serious incident may be constituted into a short-lived, firefighting team.

It must be said that this call, in particular, can create panic and additional overhead which actually slow resolution of the incident, rather than smoothing its way. This is particularly the case when senior staff on the call think they can help to resolve the incident and start to micromanage the process.

A typical standard request workflow (stability loop)

The standard request fulfilment process is still a stability loop and looks something like Figure 2.10:

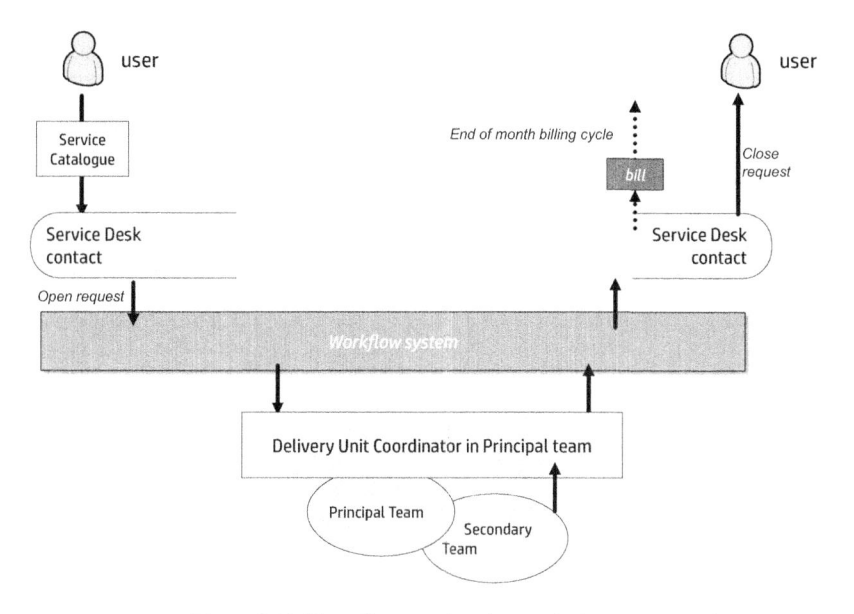

Figure 2.10 Flow diagram showing typical resource use in standard request fulfilment

Use of a single shade of grey here shows that this whole process is carried out in the support operations organisation. Although the same technical teams that were described as resolver groups in incident resolution MAY be involved, here they are described as the principal and secondary team (there may be one or more such teams for any request.

In this example, the user contacts a service desk contact and makes a request from the service catalogue. The service desk enters the request into the workflow system and this is picked up by a delivery coordinator in the principal team tasked with fulfilling the request – they then coordinate the stages of fulfilment by the principal and secondary teams and, once complete, feed this information back into the workflow system. This is picked up by the service desk staff who notify the user. Every month the client/host department is billed.

As with incidents, there are many variations on this theme. Without detailing them all, an obvious one is the full automation of the user catalogue, contact

Reframing ITIL

and workflow which feeds the requests straight to the principal and then secondary teams.

A simple non-standard request workflow (adaptability loop)

The non-standard request fulfilment process is, by definition, not standardised and many organisations don't recognise it as a distinct type. It is an adaptability loop rather than a stability loop and could look like this:

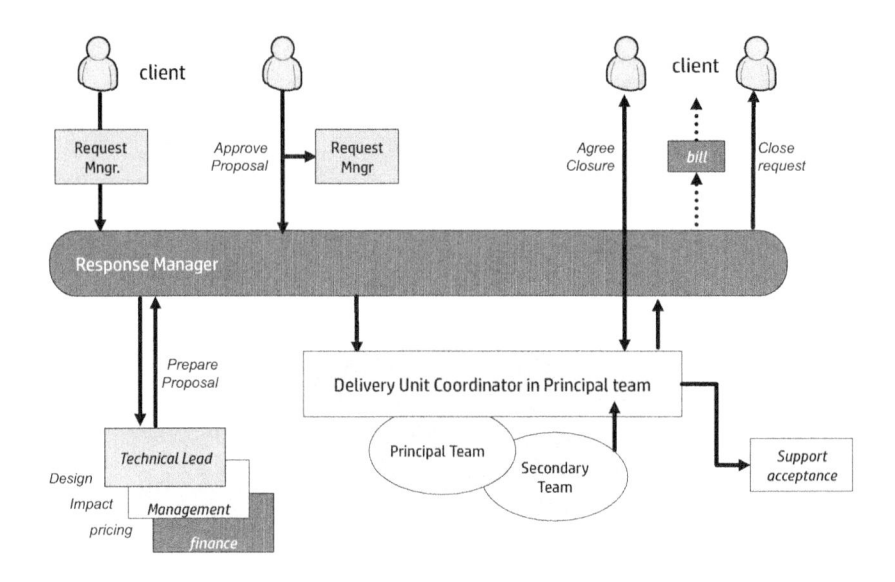

Figure 2.11 Flow diagram showing typical resource use in non-standard request fulfilment

Instead of using the service desk previously discussed, for non-standard requests there is a different triage process. This may be constituted as a dedicated triage team including some or all of the request manager, response manager and delivery unit coordinators. In some cases, dedicated technical leads, impact assessors and pricing managers may also be included. It is equally common for most of these resources to be in separate groups.

The key features of the process as shown are not the use of a request manager or response manager, which are optional, but the preparation of a proposal in response to the request which is used as the basis of approval by the client. Later, the client has to agree closure and the support organisation has to accept

Chapter 2 – Organising to Support the Service

the output (so they can support it going forward). Change management will also have been involved, although not shown here. The details can be infinitely variable.

The process shown here is for a simple non-standard request – a more complex one might also involve a project manager and a far more complex process for fulfilment.

The ITIL frame

It is useful to revisit which processes have been covered so far in this chapter and the last (Chapter 1) from the full ITIL 3 diagram introduced in the introduction- Figure 2.12.

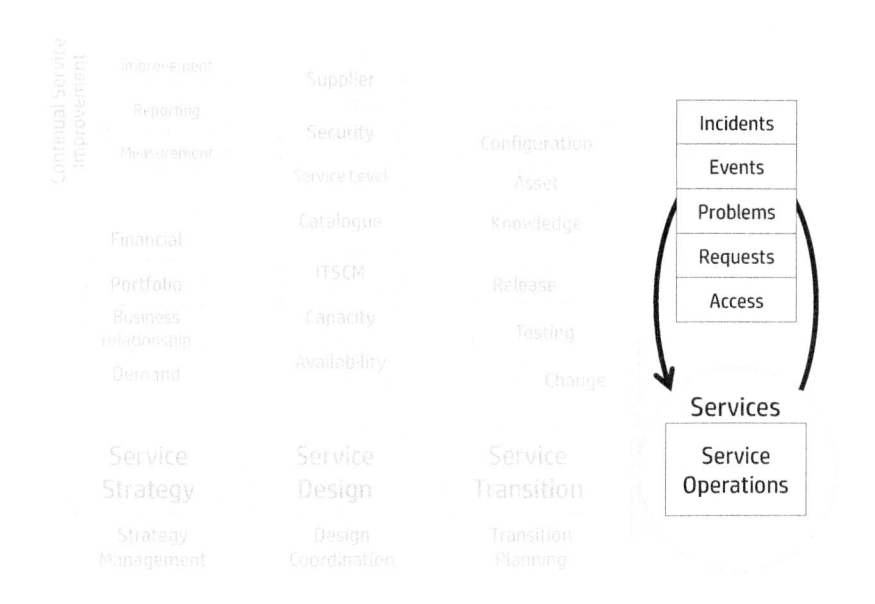

Figure 2.12 Service operations processes in the ITIL 3 frame

It is fairly clear here that there is a good match between ITIL 3's definition of Service Operation processes and the ones considered here. Further, it is reassuring to note that they are, indeed, really all processes. The significance of this becomes clearer later as other processes do not always match so straightforwardly onto the various parts (systems) of IT support organisations.

Reframing ITIL

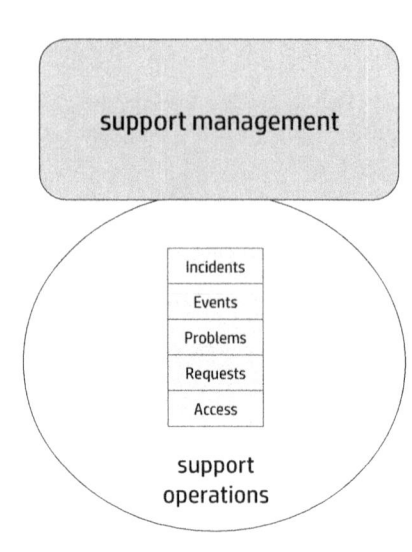

```
┌─────────────────────────────┐
│    support management       │
└─────────────────────────────┘
        ┌─────────────┐
       │  Incidents   │
       │  Events      │
       │  Problems    │
       │  Requests    │
       │  Access      │
        │   support    │
        │  operations  │
        └─────────────┘
```

Figure 2.13 ITIL support processes in the simple organisational model

It is also worth showing these ITIL support processes fitting into the organisation, although it is not the most informative of diagrams at this stage (Figure 2.13). Problem management may stray into the development operations group as well – not shown here.

This makes more sense later in the book (especially Chapters 4 and 5) when other processes are shown against the same organisational model.

Please also remember that there are a number of processes including non-standard requests and service lifecycle processes that *ought* to be here, but which are not full ITIL processes.

Chapter 3

Developing the Service

Service development was briefly introduced in the last chapter which then went on to focus on service support. Here we will look again at service development. However, it is not the intention of this chapter to describe service development – and its two ITIL components, Service Design and Service Transition – in great detail. More, it is our intention to place them in context so that their significance is clear and the issues around them are revealed.

To be treated as an operational component of the service management organisation, development has to be something that the organisation can get paid for, and this is certainly the case. For outsourced IT, this is nearly always the case and, even in in-house IT, funds would normally be charged and transferred for service development.

ITIL does not attempt to specify or proscribe particular project or programme management methodologies for service development. However, because of its existence within the UK government framework, for waterfall development it is implicit that PRINCE2® (project management) and MSP® (programme management) would be compatible with ITIL development projects. Indeed, many aspects of the Service Transition block assume an overriding waterfall approach. In particular, the service design pack concept introduced as part of Service Design makes this assumption. Unfortunately, although it is meant to be project management methodology agnostic, ITIL 3 was not designed with more recent development methodologies, such as Agile and DevOps, in mind. It looks as though ITIL 4 may be different in this. Some of the issues regarding ITIL and Agile and DevOps in particular, will be discusssed in brief at the end of this chapter.

PRINCE2® and MSP® are (registered) Trade Marks of AXELOS Limited. All rights reserved.

The organisational frame

In service support the operational elements are the technology groups. However, in service development, the operational elements are projects. This does not alter the fundamental structure of a management group sitting with an operations group which contains the projects – see Figure 3.1. Projects are just as much organisational units with the feature that they are (in most cases!) temporary structures with a defined lifetime; while they are happening they definitely behave as organisational units.

Projects have all the components of management and operations that would be expected and which are discussed in more detail in Chapter 4. This is additional to starts and ends and a number of reasonably defined stages and elements. For IT development, ITIL doesn't specify many of these but leaves the project manager to follow the other methodologies already mentioned which assume a waterfall approach.

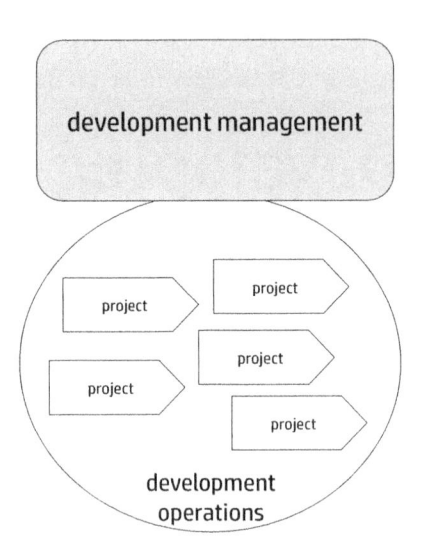

Figure 3.1 A simple organisational model showing projects as operational elements

Projects and programmes

Although the project is mainly carried out in development operations, like most operational activities it starts in development management (Figure 3.2). In fact, higher levels of management are often involved in selecting projects or designing programmes. This can be done as part of Service Strategy and/or may be selection from the Continuous Improvement (CI) register.

All three types of transformation projects introduced in Chapter 1 may be considered together for prioritisation: improvement projects, transformation requests and renewal programmes.

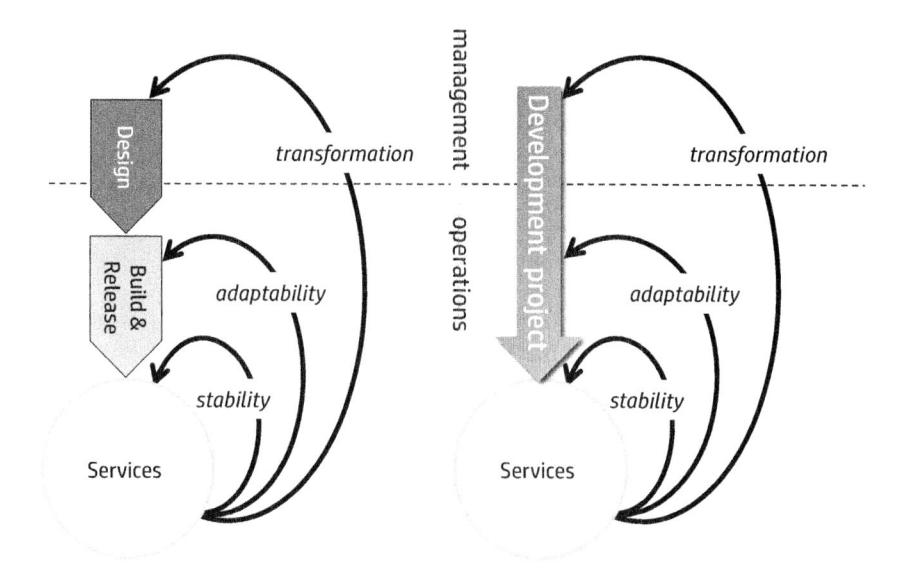

Figure 3.2 Where development projects fit with service management loops

At the management level, Service Design considers the new or revised service in the context of the whole service provided. A 'high level design' document is produced and there would often be a decision taken after this before the project 'proper' is funded and initiated. It is at this stage that the client (internal or external) would agree to pay for the service development and this initiates the start of the true development stage.

Following this, typically a project manager would be appointed who, with appropriate assistance from a project management office (PMO), acts as the management of the particular project.

Other projects are much simpler and arise from adaptability (or even, rarely, stability) loops. In this case the issue is often one of size rather than complexity and significant design input may not be required. An example would be the sourcing, delivery and setup of a large number of personal computers for a client. In this case higher management input would be minimal.

Reframing ITIL

The ITIL frame

Looking from the perspective of the ITIL 3 framework, project elements are derived mainly from the Service Transition block, with some from the Service Design block. This is shown in the general ITIL diagram introduced in the introduction, but showing here only the processes relevant to operations in development – Figure 3.3.

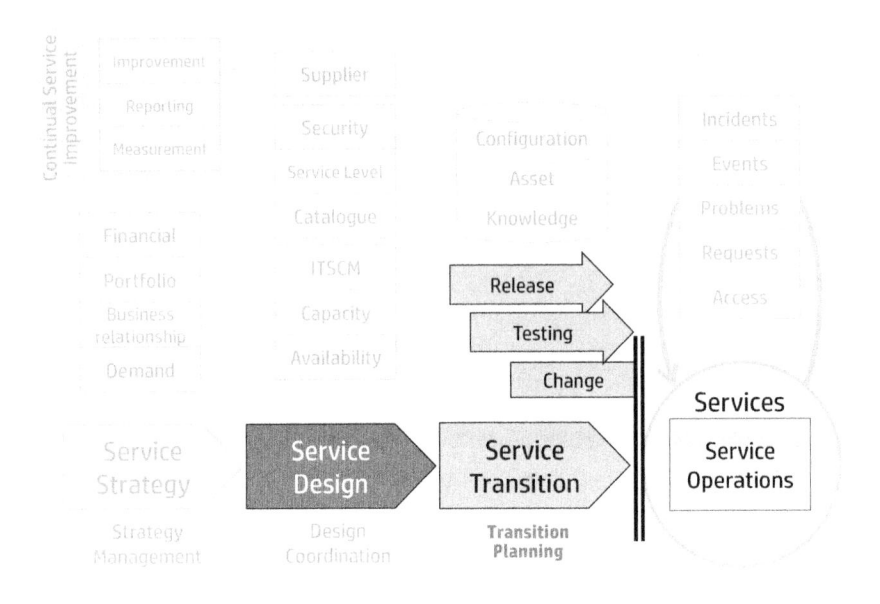

Figure 3.3 Service development processes in the ITIL 3 frame

Only some of the Service Transition 'processes' are included since the others are found to be part of managing a service – see Chapters 4 & 5. Service Design is invoked, but none of the processes included in it are deemed to be operational – these are also found to be part of management. Indeed, it is the coordination process encompassed in the Service Design pack that is most relevant. 'Build' is entirely missing in the ITIL 2 & 3 canon but is found in ITIL 4. Note that change evaluation is here considered as an integral part of change.

ITIL processes in service development operations

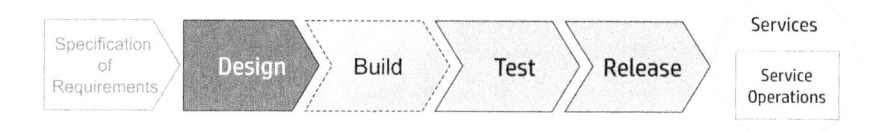

Figure 3.4 Linear representation of service development

Although really half of a (transformation) loop – see Figure 3.2 – the basic service development process can be shown as linear (Figure 3.4) and follows a straightforward sequence in its simplest form with four clear stages. To this can be added a fifth stage at the beginning: the 'set-up' stage of obtaining requirements or providing a specification – something in which the customer, whether internal or a business client, is closely consulted.

As ITIL defines these processes, they are not entirely sequential (Figure 3.5). In particular the release and deployment process is seen to oversee the service testing and validation process as well as deployment and early-life support. Further, the change management process anticipates and controls the change to the live service resulting from release. This is focused towards the later stages of the project.

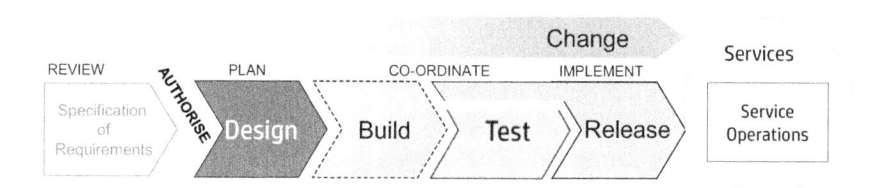

Figure 3.5 ITIL processes in service development

Controls described in Service Design in the early stages define the impact of the project, usually in a strategic context – with a focus on business need, cost and wider impact. Finally, Evaluation is a methodology used mainly during the review of a proposed change prior to transition.

As can be seen from the shadings used, most of these processes are described in ITIL 3 as being in Service Transition (the lighter grey).

Service Design

In ITIL 3, the Service Design process is one of the larger disciplines in its own right. Intriguingly, Service Design does not feature itself as one of its own processes in ITIL 3 (the emphasis is different in ITIL 4), although there is much useful guidance on what should be included. The key point is the need to have a holistic view of the package of services provided and all aspects of the links in between them. Many of the aspects that should be considered have their own processes and according to ITIL 3 are owned in Service Design.

Service Design is frequently carried out by a group of service architects who may work at different levels of service complexity – from overarching strategic design for the Service Strategy group, right down to detailed design of processes, code or equipment.

Build

Although three of the service development stages are clearly found in ITIL 3, this second stage, 'build', is missing as an explicit process although it is described in Service Transition. This has sometimes reduced the credibility of ITIL 3 – particularly with application developers for whom build is the most substantial part of their work. ITIL 4 remedies this with discussion of obtain/build.

In fairness, it must be said that there is not always a significant build stage in service development, especially if the service is infrastructure/hardware based. If the service is delivery of a commercial product, build may be selection and testing of candidate products. If the service (enhancement) is roll out of to a new geographical site, then build may be installation of cables, setting up a server centre and set up of PCs.

However, in other cases, particularly application development, build may be a substantial code writing activity involving hundreds of software engineers over several months or years. In ITIL 3, applications development options using a Waterfall or RAD (rapid application development) process are discussed in Service Design.

Service validation and testing

Testing is one of the processes in the Service Transition discipline. In ITIL 3 it is referred to as 'service validation and testing'. The purpose of testing is to ensure that the service that has already been designed and built is now 'fit for purpose'. To this end, a variety of tests are applied at a range of levels. Technical fitness is tested as well as various types of user testing.

Testing of service components should have been carried out throughout the build stages, but it is still not uncommon for services to be passed back for rebuild and, in exceptional cases, redesign, as a result of their failing at the testing stage.

Once the testing has been passed to the satisfaction of the developers and customer alike, then the service can be deployed. The relationship of testing and release is not sequential (see Figure 3.5).

Release and deployment management

Release is one of the processes in the Service Transition discipline and it works in parallel with and is closely associated with change management. In ITIL 3 it is referred to as 'release and deployment management'. The purpose of release is to ensure that the release of the new service into the live environment is trouble free. It is seen to encompass the testing processes and to manage them rather than be the next step.

Release and deployment manages the roll-out / implementation of a new service. It manages the testing through to a pilot stage in deployment and early life support in Service Operation, when unforeseen problems can occur and exceptional service support may be required. In the case where a new service replaces an old one, then the switch over and removal of the old service is also within scope.

Validation that the new service is functioning as expected is also carried out and, in hopefully rare cases, withdrawal of the service where it fails to function appropriately is managed.

Change management (and change evaluation)

As its main emphasis is on controlling change to the live service – a service management role – the change management and change evaluation processes are discussed towards the end of the next chapter – Chapter 4.

Reframing ITIL

The communications frame

For service development, the key frame which determines the success or failure, usefulness or disaster of an IT project, is communications. There are three aspects to this: intra-project communications, extra-project communications and inter-project communications.

Intra-project communication – project handover

Intra-project communications concerns communication between the parties involved in developing and supporting a service through the project stages. Indeed, the division of a service development project into four, five or more stages may already have raised an alarm – how are communications managed between the stages to ensure continuity and consistency throughout? We have already seen that Service Design starts in management before moving into a more operational space. For the intra-project communication frame it, in fact, starts earlier with the requirements, which often come out of Service Strategy. This may involve the client and perhaps another branch of management: customer/client liaison. Additionally, at the end there are also communication failures during release in the passing over of the project to service operations – these are the most agonised over as they cause the most visible problems.

If we focus on the potential points requiring special care with communications, the service development process looks more like Figure 3.6 – with pronounced gaps and each black arrow a possible cause of miscommunication. It is telling that the arrows are only pointing one way – feedback loops are rarely seen and the process flows in one direction only. After all, this is a waterfall project model and water only flows downhill.

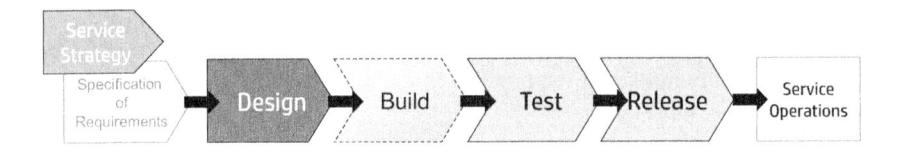

Figure 3.6 Intra-project communication through Service development

ITIL is well aware of the coordination and communications issues that this staged development creates and, in response, has created the service design pack (SDP). This starts out as a fairly thin document in requirements and grows at each stage of the project with new and enhanced sections – until eventually it has documented all the decisions and issues that the project has encountered through the five stages. The SDP, if fully implemented, is a substantial set of documents and full implementation would only be appropriate to a substantial development project. Like, everything in ITIL, it can be scaled down, but this must be done carefully or it can then lose much of its value in the process. The final service design pack is a key document and itself may be considered a part of the resulting service.

Additionally, in some organisations all these stages may be managed by a *single* project manager and support team – this is not covered by ITIL – although their grasp of the technical detail is usually weak, this makes it possible to ensure that a consistent focus on business benefit is maintained.

However, each of the stages is usually managed and performed by a different group within IT or IT management. They have different understanding, focus, expertise and motivation. Sometimes they are parts of different organisations – especially if IT is outsourced. The development may be carried out by one outsourcer and the operations (support) by another completely. This is the nightmare scenario that triggers the fears of 'throwing the development over the wall' as it goes live. It is highly unlikely that the developers' motivation to build a service would produce a service that is easy to maintain by support groups. Many decades of bad experiences have shown that this is, indeed, the case.

One of the biggest problems in managing a project like this is that the documents in the SDP, even if properly and comprehensively produced and read, can never provide the levels of insight and clarity required for anything but the most straightforward of projects.

Effective communication runs in a sequence of gradual improvement from:

documents ➔ presentations ➔ dialogue ➔ collaboration

Figure 3.7 Grades of communication quality

The last three are all face to face. Moving from left to right two things happen, the communication moves from one-directional to two-way and the richness of the communication increases (also known as increasing the variety). There is only one way to provide the best communication: collaboration

Collaboration

It is recognised amongst good service developers that early involvement of the later-stage groups (principally testing and support) improves the speed and quality of design and build. In particular, involving Service Operation staff at the design stage helps to ensure that the service will be supportable. Later involvement, well before handover, ensures that the service operations staff is ready and prepared to take over the new service. Dedicated handover teams may be involved in 'early-life' support to smooth this further. Hence collaboration is ensured. See Figure 3.8.

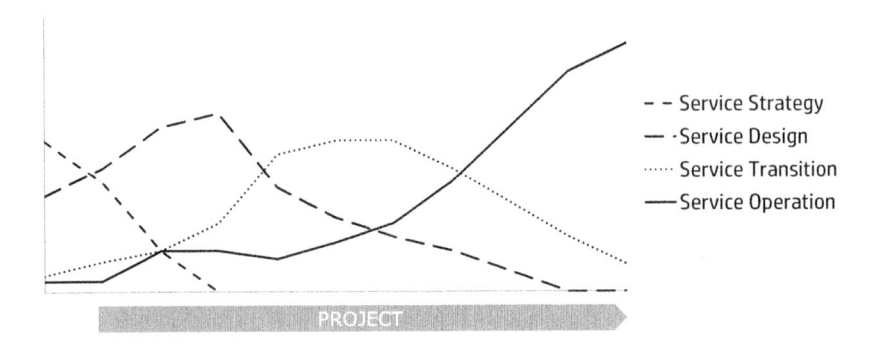

Figure 3.8 Proportion of staff from each group involved throughout a typical project

The service design pack specifies early involvement of the later groups in preparation of the document and, if followed, will encourage this.

Extra-project communication – project change

As well as communications along the project path, communications between a project and outside agencies – especially clients and other projects – are essential to keep the project focused on business benefits and the more general business, IT and IT support environments – see Figure 3.9. These are often mediated by the project manager.

From their perspective, these external communications are seen negatively as they can redirect work and add cost. Hence a change management process is used to control these inputs. ITIL's change management process is used pretty much exclusively in Service Operation to control release rather than earlier in

Chapter 3 – Developing the Service

service development. Hence the project change control required here derives almost entirely from the project management process (often PRINCE2) being employed.

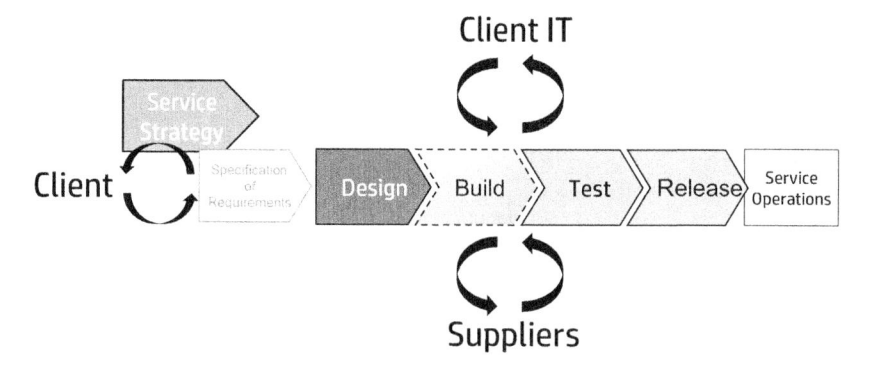

Figure 3.9 Extra-project communications during service development

Unfortunately, if the client does need or want changes, too tight a control on changes to the project requirements or details reduces the relevance of the development. To ensure this doesn't happen, governance of the project, programmes and portfolio need to be managed between the developers and client. This is important regardless of whether the developers are internal or outsourced.

A particularly useful approach to this is ladder governance – also mentioned in Chapter 7 – which allows issues to be resolved at the lowest possible level and only issues that cannot be so resolved are escalated to higher rungs on the governance ladder (Figure 3.10). This makes for an effective use of project and other management time and ensures that client/developer issues – large and small – all get covered at the level of detail they require.

An example of joint project/programme governance
IT project managers would normally hold at least weekly 'project team meetings' with the equivalent client project managers. Each project manager would respectively report progress internally to the IT department, to their programme managers, who then also meet weekly in the 'programme leadership team meeting'.

The same people meet monthly, perhaps also with the business unit programme delivery manager, in a 'programme review' meeting, where similar and major issues are discussed. Above this level there may be a less frequent portfolio

Reframing ITIL

review meeting and perhaps a review of the full development portfolio at the executive level. These meetings are often less formal and arise as required.

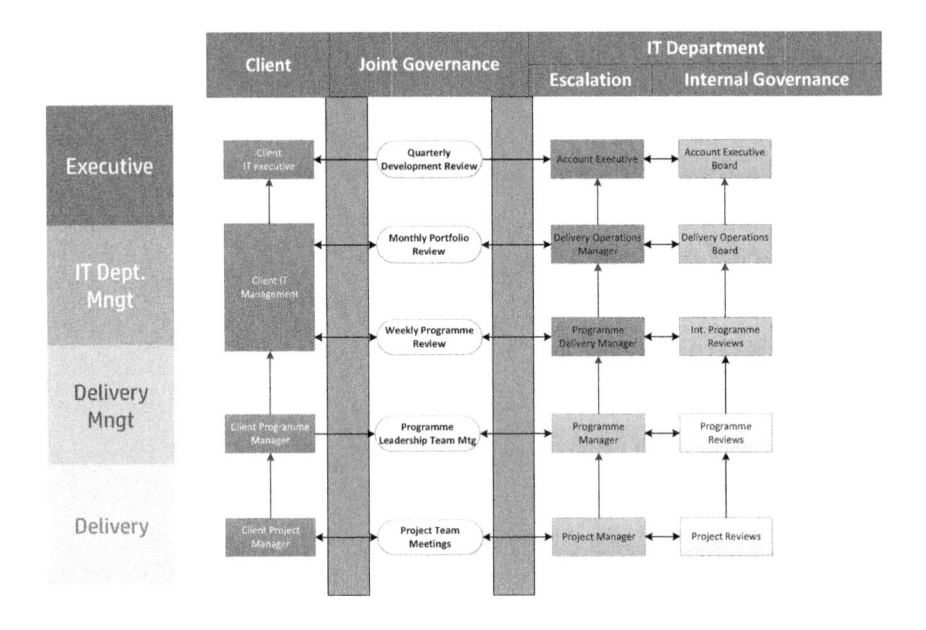

Figure 3.10 Ladder governance showing reporting lines and escalation routes

Aligned with these joint meetings are escalation routes internal to the IT development department: Here, escalations pass from the project manager, to the programme manager, to the programme delivery manager, and so on up the management chain.

Inter-project communication – interactions and complexity

In large, interacting, multi-project environments something else happens: the projects can have an impact on each other. A delay or change in one knocks on to the other projects that are linked. This can occur at almost any stage of any of the projects as shown in Figure 3.11.

Chapter 3 – Developing the Service

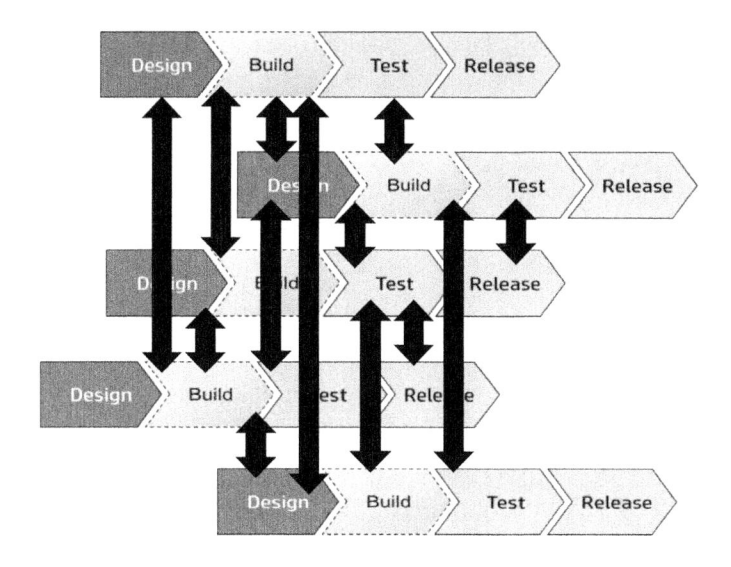

Figure 3.11 Multiple points of inter-project interactions

The number of possible interactions increases in a triangular series each time a new project is added as shown in Table 3.1.

No. of projects	No of additional interactions	Total no. of interactions
1	0	0
2	1	1
3	2	3
4	3	6
5	4	10
6	5	15
7	6	21
8	7	28

Table 3.1 Increase in number of interactions as the total number of projects increases

In this case with only eight projects running together, there are 28 possible interactions. Adding a ninth project would increase this by a further eight possible interactions and so forth. Each time a change occurs in one of the

Reframing ITIL

projects, all the other linked projects have to (should) assess any likely impact on their own project. In Figure 3.12 each project is shown as a single blob to simplify the diagram:

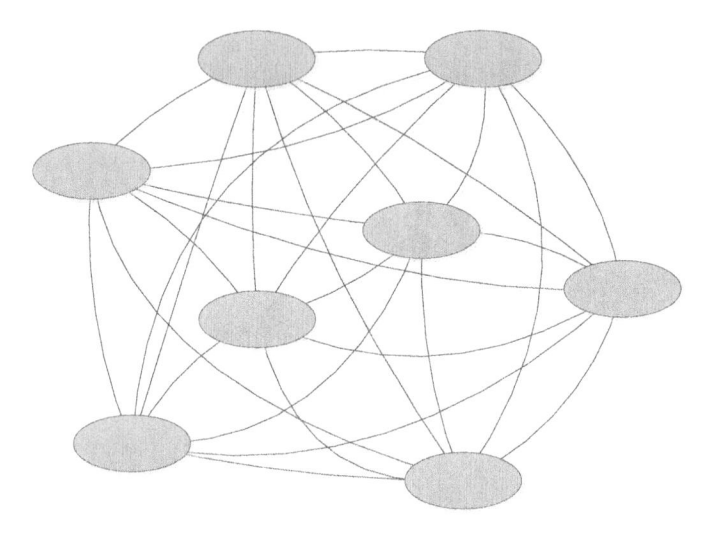

Figure 3.12 Possible interactions between eight parallel projects

Although all the possible interactions are shown – and note that these are two-way – in reality the real number of dependencies would be fewer as some projects cannot have any dependency on another. If all the possible dependencies were real, then a change in any one project would delay ALL the other projects, and this doesn't happen.

Trying to control this many possible interactions is a serious challenge to project and programme managers who may be responsible. If there are too many actual dependencies something that is often unexpected happens: the interactions take over the programme and the whole thing grinds to a halt resulting in massive delays. There is a scientific principle behind this described by Christopher Alexander in his book *Notes on the Synthesis of Form*.

An effective way round this is to group the projects into manageable chunks – programmes – of inter-dependent projects and then manage the dependencies *within* the chunks and separately manage the dependencies *between* the chunks – see Figure 3.13. If managed intelligently and consistently, this can reduce the dependencies to a point where the overall portfolio of programmes doesn't grind to a halt. In the example shown the total possible interactions are reduced

Chapter 3 – Developing the Service

from a potential 190 to 47 and the maximum within any one group to 15 (when there are six projects in a programme).

Sadly there are a number of well-known examples of large government projects where this was not done successfully and was one of the reasons that millions of pounds – even billions – were wasted.

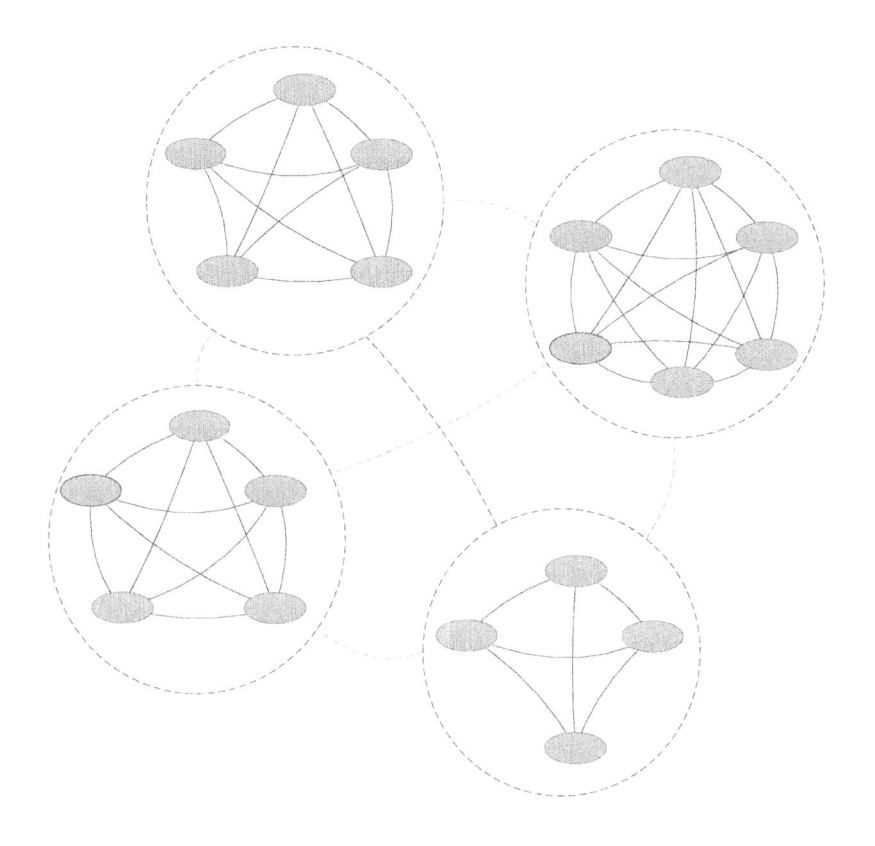

Figure 3.13 Reducing the number of interactions between twenty projects by grouping them into four programmes

In very practical terms, the way to manage projects and programmes together is to hold a series of regular reviews between client and project and programme teams at different levels in the organisation. This is again, ladder governance (Figure 3.10) and is designed to ensure that only issues that need to be escalated are escalated. This makes it possible to manage the complexity of large numbers of projects constituted in programmes and programme portfolios.

Agile and DevOps

Agile and DevOps represent two, non-waterfall, ways of developing software projects. Both have evolved mainly for the application development space rather than other types of projects.

In ITIL 2 and 3 these are not mentioned or considered, however ITIL 4 does incorporate them and encourages their use. It is not the purpose of this book to explain how Agile and DevOps work, but it is worth considering how they help resolve some of the difficulties with waterfall project development that have been discussed above.

Although they do much more, both these approaches resolve issues in the communication frame, but in different aspects:

Agile focuses on resolving client/developer extra-project communications and DevOps (short for Development/Operations) focuses on resolving developer/support (i.e. handover) intra-project communications. There is no doubt that from the perspective of knowledge sharing, both approaches are excellent.

Agile
Agile is a rapid application development (RAD) methodology and it ensures that change is designed in – a close relationship is ensured between the client and developer and the project produces frequent, relatively small, releases to live that allow the users to try out the new service (usually software) and feedback any improvement or requirements. This is usually done within an iterative framework where requirements and solutions may evolve – the emphasis is on speedy development. This is the antithesis of the waterfall approach.

Teams are multi-disciplinary and co-located – further, all team members are encouraged to develop multi-disciplinary skills so that when something needs fixing, almost anyone can do it. In large programme environments the interactions between projects can be a problem and many of the issues discussed in Chapter 6 – regarding the strengths and weaknesses of various organisational models – arise.

Chapter 3 – Developing the Service

DevOps

DevOps on the other hand resolves the developer/support issues already discussed above. It is nearly always combined with an Agile approach, with frequent, relatively small, releases to live. However, the emphasis is on reliability rather than speed. DevOps teams include developers and support staff – collaboration is strongly emphasised. One area of focus is the integration of specialists who focus on putting software onto infrastructure. DevOps specialists may operate in parallel with software developers and specialist support staff. However, in some cases the developers also carry out the support when the DevOps team has the responsibility for both software development and support.

DevOps can be seen as similar to the old approach of developers doing support which was common before standardised processes such as ITIL were introduced. It can suffer from the same issues of many developers not wanting to do support and/or support requirements overwhelming them and not allowing time for development.

ITIL, Agile and DevOps

So, are Agile and DevOps incompatible with ITIL? This has often been claimed but with their focus on the development process (which ITIL doesn't cover, even for waterfall methodologies – implying the use of PRINCE2 / MSP or similar) there is actually not a large area of conflict.

- There would still be a need for incident and problem management processes.

- Change, release and testing management need to be handled *very* differently in both cases, but are still essential.

- Staff organisation and skill sets would be differently allocated within teams and elsewhere – but this is not a key issue for ITIL.

- Other supporting processes discussed later in Chapters 4 and 5 are largely still required as they are fundamental to the organisation of IT support and development.

It is the view of the authors that although ITIL would need considerable adaptation in the operational support and development spaces, it is still sufficiently 'project methodology agnostic' to be highly relevant. DevOps and

Reframing ITIL

Agile may be seen as effective ways of solving respectively the intra-project and extra-project communication problems found in any software development. ITIL 4 goes some way towards finding ways that ITIL, Agile and DevOps can work together.

The Organisational frame

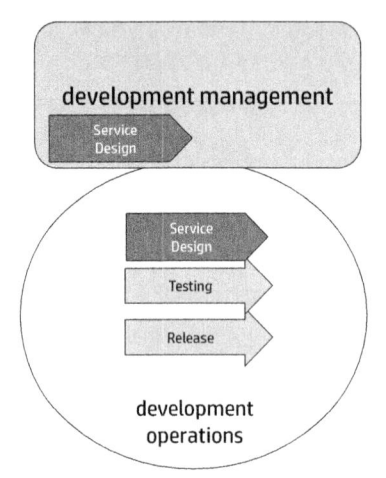

Figure 3.14 ITIL development processes in the simple organisational model

It is again worth showing where the ITIL development processes fit into the organisation, as was done in Chapter 2 and will also be done in Chapters 4 and 5.

It is notable that only two actual 'processes', and part of Service Design, are to be found in service development operations.

The rest of the processes here are to be found in other project and programme methodologies – such as PRINCE2, MSP, or even Agile and DevOps.

Chapter 4

Managing the Service

So far in Chapters 1 to 3 we have looked at operational processes which actually look like processes: they describe events and actions that may branch or circle back but which are essentially sequential. In Chapters 4 and 5 we are going to look at processes which often internally demonstrate sequences of events, but which sit in management. In order to do make some sense of these we need a model of organisation that lets us pull these processes apart and see what they do in management terms. We will use a well-established systems thinking model of the organisation – the viable system model, developed by Stafford Beer. All these processes are part of managing the service and its supporting organisation.

The ITIL frame

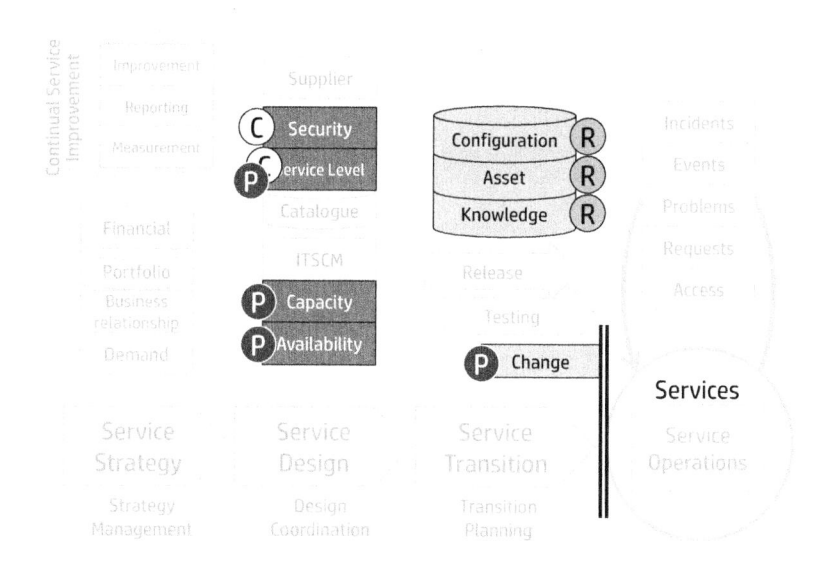

Figure 4.1 ITIL 3 processes considered in Chapter 4

Reframing ITIL

Referring back to the ITIL 3 process diagram first shown in the introduction, we will be addressing a subset of those processes here. The ones in question – those particularly appropriate for managing the service – are highlighted in Figure 4.1. It may be noted that they do not group well with the ITIL 3 divisions into 'books' or disciplines. This is because the ITIL grouping is not based in ITSM organisational structures. One purpose of this chapter is to remedy that.

The groupings and shapes used for the processes in this diagram also have some meaning. For example the configuration, asset and knowledge management processes are all shown in the shape traditionally used for databases – this is because these are essentially repositories, also hence the **R**. Further, only three: capacity, availability and change management, are really processes (**P**). Security and service level management are capabilities (**C**). Change evaluation is included here as part of change management as it is entirely subservient to it.

Let us now look at each of these 'processes' in some more detail to help us understand their role and context in managing the service. To do this we need to add some detail to the organisational diagram first introduced in Chapter 2 by introducing several additional management systems:

The organisational frame

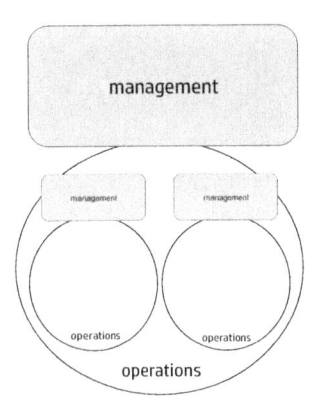

Figure 4.2 More detail of management processes at the Service level (see text for explanation)

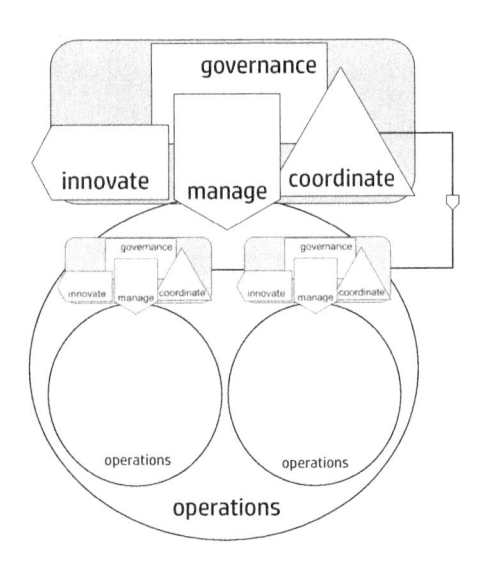

Chapter 4 – Managing the Service

The simple organisational structure that was previously shown as management and operations, then with lower levels nested within it, must now be expanded to begin to explain the underlying systems, or activities that make up management. A further discussion of this can be found in Chapter 7.

As we are now focusing on management, operations stays as it was and contains only the lower level-management/operations activities. The RH side of Figure 4.2 shows two levels in the organisation – the higher level corresponding to the service. Above this is another level (not shown) corresponding to the whole IT support organisation – which may be an outsourced account or an in-house IT department. The next chapter (5) focuses on processes associated with this level and Figure 5.3 shows more organisational levels.

When considering the *innovation* (or *innovate*), *management* (or *manage*), *governance* and *coordination* (or *coordinate*) activities, please do note that there is no implication that each of these activities has its own, discrete department. In fact, the departments found in normal management frequently carry out several of these activities: for example, a finance department will manage the organisation's finances (*management*), forecast projected finances (*innovation*) and provide financial standards to the organisation (*coordination*).

Management (manage)

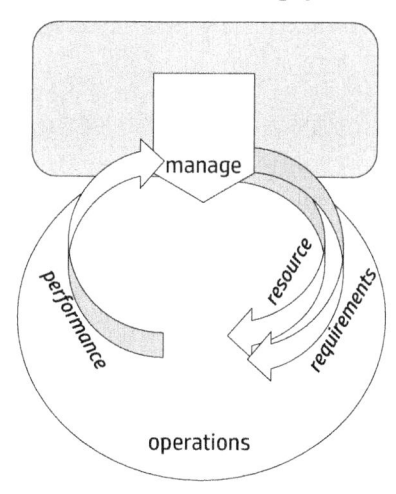

Figure 4.3 The *management* system at a single level in an organisation

Management need a system for directing and requesting work, for providing the resource for that work and for measuring how well it is being done. This is well understood and is what most people probably think of as management. It will be referred to here as the *management* system (Figure 4.3).

Management includes activities that are known as resource negotiation. This describes provision of resource to ensure that a certain level of performance can be achieved – without the resource, performance will certainly be lower.

63

This simple and obvious relationship seems to have been lost in a surprisingly large number of organisations. There is considerable inflexibility built in, additionally, by annual budgeting cycles, which frequently results in organisations committing to customer demand levels that they simply fail to resource.

Coordination (coordinate)

A second system that management needs is one that provides standards and practices for the subsidiary groups to use to make sure that they all work in an aligned and joined-up way. This reduces the tendency for teams or departments to 'go their own way' – each developing their own preferred ways of doing things.

This will be referred to as the *coordination* system (Figure 4.4).

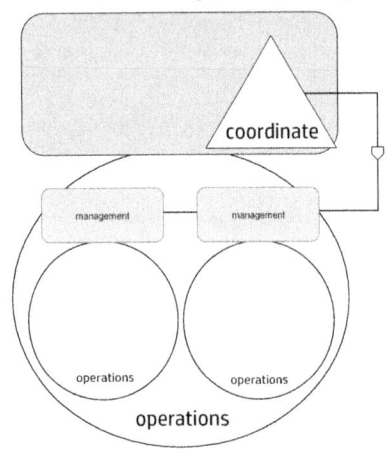

Figure 4.4 The *coordination* system at a single level in an organisation

This tends to come in two forms: For the more complicated issues, meetings are organised to ensure that subsidiary groups are aligned – some negotiation is inevitable. For more straightforward and usually more frequent issues — standards are provided.

Meetings can include group board meetings, quality meetings, interdepartmental liaison and so forth, and standards can include schedules, financial reporting standards, process standards, timetables, handover criteria, salary policy – the list is almost endless.

Innovation (innovate)

The *management* system (and also the *coordination* system, mostly) focus on the organisation as it is now, on making sure it is delivering what is required. However all organisations also need to plan for the future, look out for what is coming from outside, ensure that there is research and development going on, and that development is responding effectively to changing demand from the service provider's marketplace and clients. This will be referred to as the *innovation* system (Figure 4.5).

Chapter 4 – Managing the Service

In IT this function is fulfilled by three groups:

1. The architects who are looking for new technology initiatives – from both inside the main outsourcing organisation and also from suppliers.

2. Sales or business relationship managers, by whatever name – who look into requirements from, or possibilities in the client business. In both cases the aim would be to generate new programmes of work to bring new services to the client.

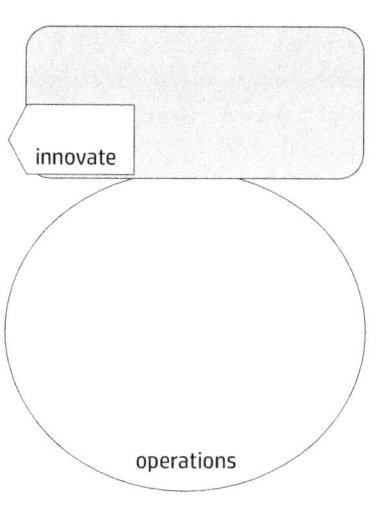

Figure 4.5 The *innovation* system at a single level in an organisation

3. The improvement group who are looking for opportunities to improve existing services through reorganisation, redefinition of processes, revised services, new tooling etc. Again the aim is to get the client to approve new work programmes. In exceptional cases where reduced costs are expected, the outsourced service provider could provide the resourcing itself.

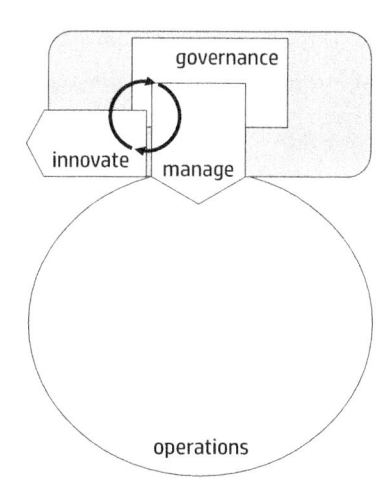

Figure 4.6 The *governance* system at a single level in an organisation

Governance

Governance is the final management system we are going to describe here. Its purpose is to keep the *innovation* and *management* systems in balance. When we consider that the *management* system is to keep the business focused on the present and on successful delivery, whereas the *innovation* system is focused on the future and making sure the business is prepared for that, the importance of maintaining this balance becomes clear.

There are many examples of businesses that have focused on efficiency (*management*) and ignored *innovation* and have then been tripped up by technology changes or competitors changing their businesses. There are fewer example of the reverse, but some businesses – particularly in digital technologies – are suffering from this.

Resource types

A number of types of resource are used in any organisation and are particularly discussed as part of the *management* system. However, in this context, resource goes beyond just financial resource although finance is required to provide each of these – perhaps at some remove.

In IT organisations the important additional resources may be described as

1. people and capabilities
2. specialist infrastructure – hardware and software
3. facilities
4. know-how

We will now look at each of the management systems in the context of ITIL processes that manage the service.

ITIL 'processes' by management system

The organisational frame shows how an organisation works, so if a process is not part of an operational loop (Chapters 1 and 3) whether support, delivery or development – it must fit into one or more of these management systems.

Investigating how the processes fit with these management systems is key to understanding the organisational role of ITIL processes and to identifying what may be missing.

Management – the resource negotiation loop
The following processes contain mostly activities that fit into the system we have called *management* and which encompasses the resource negotiation loop:

Capacity and availability management
Capacity and availability management [Service Design] are a closely related pair of mainly *management* processes. Both are mainly concerned with the

Chapter 4 – Managing the Service

allocation of the specialist infrastructure resource type to services and its measurement.

Capacity and availability management are often described as being two sides of the same coin: this is in fact a fairly accurate description. Capacity is sometimes described as capacity and performance which interestingly indicates its role in the performance measurement part of the infrastructure resource negotiation.

An examination of the purpose of both 'processes' shows that they produce resource plans and define and manage requirements. They also then measure the actual performance and modify the resource and plans accordingly. This is almost a classic description of the resource management loop and is shown in Figure 4.7.

Other subsidiary activities for capacity and availability management include assisting with the resolution of incidents and problems – an *operational* activity – and making input to the assessment of the impact of changes – a *coordination* activity.

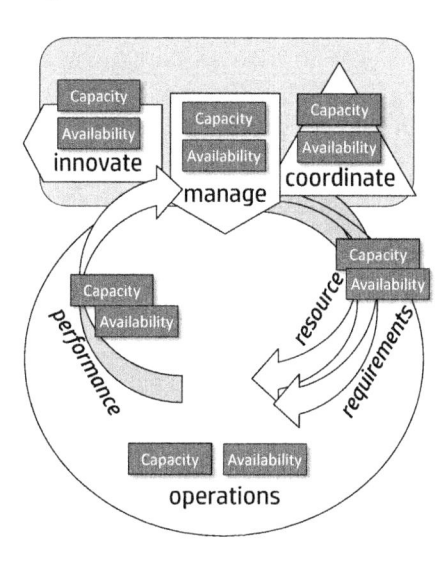

Figure 4.7 Capacity and availability Management mapped onto the *management* resource negotiation loop

Ensuring that proactive measures to improve performance and capacity are implemented are *innovation* activities. All of these activities take place at the service level in the organisation. So it can be seen that these two closely related processes whose pre-eminent role is resource negotiation, include a rounded set of activities, albeit entirely regarding specialist infrastructure.

Reframing ITIL

> ### *What is capacity management?*
> Capacity management essentially begins with the monitoring of all types of physical and virtual capacity in an IT service, e.g. transmission, servers, applications, and the extent to which they are being 'consumed', or might theoretically be consumed in order to service the organisation and its customers. Effective capacity management will have thresholds set for analysis, planning, investment, build, and at the other extreme, disposal. It is vital that capacity management is firmly interlocked with financial, strategic, marketing and operational practices, with which it shares data.
>
> ### *What is availability management?*
> Availability management essentially drives procedures for the minimisation of outage duration and arguably the maximisation of time between outages that effect the organisation and its customers. Accurate measurement is vital to availability management, as is the ability to monitor availability at a number of different levels, e.g. the organisation itself, as well as a customer's IT estate, without confusion about the impact of outages on that physical and virtual estate.

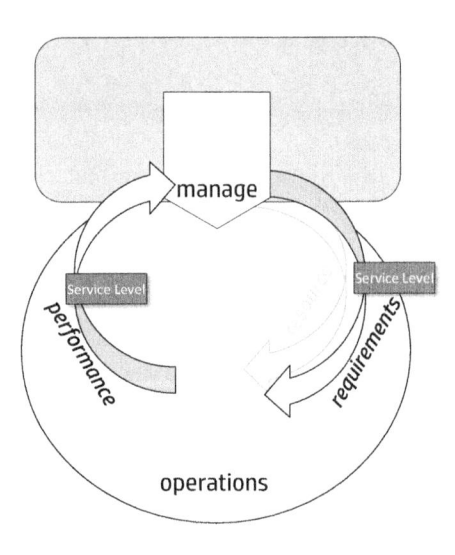

Figure 4.8 Service level management mapped onto the *management* resource negotiation loop

Service level management

Service level management or SLM [Service Design] is a process with a different focus, which is in the definition of expected service performance and then monitoring and reporting the actual service performance. As well as the performance of the specialist infrastructure – some of which overlaps with the capacity and availability processes – the performance of another resource type, people, is also included. This is principally in the form of how well staff perform in contact, incident and resource resolution.

Service level management therefore has a strong role in the performance side of the resource negotiation loop. It also helps to define the performance requirements on the other side of the loop; however, it has no direct role in

68

Chapter 4 – Managing the Service

resourcing. If everything is to work well, then the performance levels need to inform other parts of management to adjust resource accordingly.

Service level management also has roles in reporting the performance right up the management chain to the parent business (or client business if IT is outsourced). The desired service levels are negotiated with the client business (or between the IT Department and the rest of the business if IT support is in-house) and performance against the service levels is also reported back through the same route. This actually occurs at a higher level in the organisation than the service, but via the same resource negotiation route in *management*.

The right service level?

Although service levels are often based on standards used throughout the industry, it is still essential to understand exactly what is being measured and how this drives behaviour. There is a temptation on the part of the client/business to drive extremely rapid responses for (e.g.) fixing incidents even when there is no business justification. This can result in unnecessarily high cost and/or drive repeated failures to meet the unrealistic service levels. Similarly overambitious service levels can be set for technical responses in the infrastructure, with similar knock-on effects on cost and failure.

Information security management

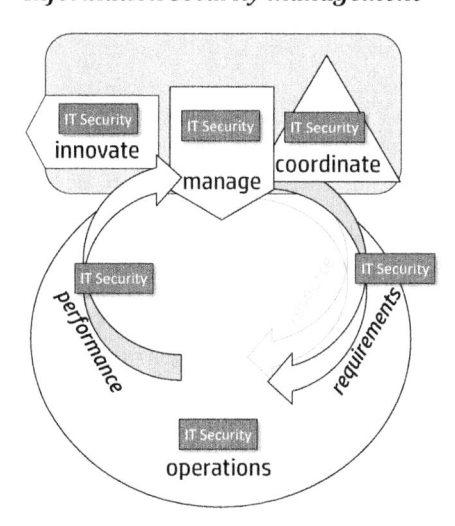

Figure 4.9 Information security management mapped onto the *management* resource negotiation loop

Information security management [Service Design] permeates the whole organisation from policy setting to managing accesses – logical and physical. It is more an organisational capability than a process and is perpetuated by *management* at all levels of the organisation.

As well as dealing with security of the specialist IT infrastructure, information security management also covers the security of know-how, facilities and people. Thus uniquely it deals with all the non-financial resource types.

Reframing ITIL

> **Examples of security**
> Physical security designed to protect infrastructure such as server farms, transmission cables, and interconnection nodes.
>
> Virtual security designed to protect applications and data, such as firewalls, encryption and sophisticated access controls.

As with service level management, security policies are derived from the parent business (or client business if IT is outsourced) – through the same route. This is emphasised in the role of information security management as aligning IT security with business security.

Information security management sits firmly in *management* where policies are produced and documented and breaches are managed. However, assistance is also given to the resolution of security incidents and problems – an *operational* activity, and to the impact of changes – a *coordination* activity. Understanding future security requirements sits in *innovation*. This time we have a rounded 'process' but without any resource provision (Figure 4.9).

The *management* role of information security management works through the resource negotiation loop with the distribution of security policy and the implementation of security controls, through requirements. Adherence to security policies is then monitored, through performance. As with service level management, there is no direct role in resource provision to support security policies, so information security management must function by informing other parts of *management* to adjust resource accordingly when required.

In *operations* in delivery and development, information security management also directly guides the access management process described in Chapter 1 which is a special security process in request fulfilment.

Service asset, configuration and knowledge management

Asset management and configuration management [Service Transition] were later grouped together by ITIL 3 as 'service asset and configuration management' and may be seen, along with knowledge management [Service Transition], as a set of repositories of know-how pertaining to services and other components – including users.

Describing knowledge management, in particular, as a repository may seem somewhat controversial. However, the descriptions in ITIL 3 make it clear that, here, knowledge management is not about a cultural issue, or the promulgation of knowledge of different types and characteristics but simply describes an information storage and retrieval system.

Chapter 4 – Managing the Service

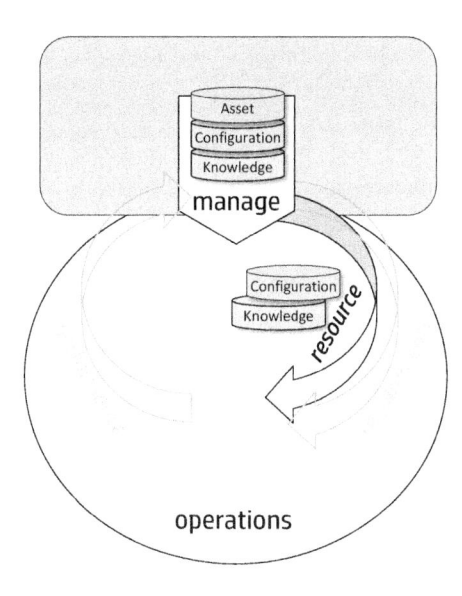

Figure 4.10 Asset, Configuration and knowledge management mapped onto the *management* resource negotiation loop

This book is probably not the right place to get into an extended discussion of how to do knowledge management or even what it is. However, the authors would recommend anyone interested to look at the work of the late Max Boisot which challenges some of the common assumptions about knowledge and information management from a systemic perspective.

Knowledge and configuration management in particular, are resources of the know-how type, relating to specialist IT infrastructure, provided to the *operations* groups to help them function. No requirements or performance measures are associated directly with these (Figure 4.10). The processes associated with them are essentially to do with maintaining the repositories and keeping them up to date and accurate (Figure 4.12).

Using configuration and knowledge management
Configuration management is particularly valuable when causes of incidents are not immediately obvious. A good configuration management system shows all the links between the components and leads the investigator on to the next most likely cause.

Knowledge management is perhaps more useful for the service desk to find previous comments about a question being raised (including incidents) and help them respond. It can also help incident and problem investigators to see what has been done before.

Poor configuration management can result in increased costs when trying to resolve incidents or problems as an investigation of the IT configuration has to take place each time. However, good configuration management and maintenance of configuration management systems is seen as an overhead and

Reframing ITIL

there is often insufficient investment by the IT department or supplier. This is a short-term view on their part.

Asset management, although also used in *operations*, has a stronger direct role in the management of the specialist IT infrastructure.

Poor asset management can also result in increased costs if the service provider cannot keep track of stock. There is another problem if we think of staff as assets – in particular regarding contractors: it can sometimes be hard to keep track of contractors!

abstraction ↑	Finance	Numbers combining things in the real world
	Asset	Names and quantities of things in the real world
	Configuration	Model of things and relationships in the real world
	Service	**The real world**

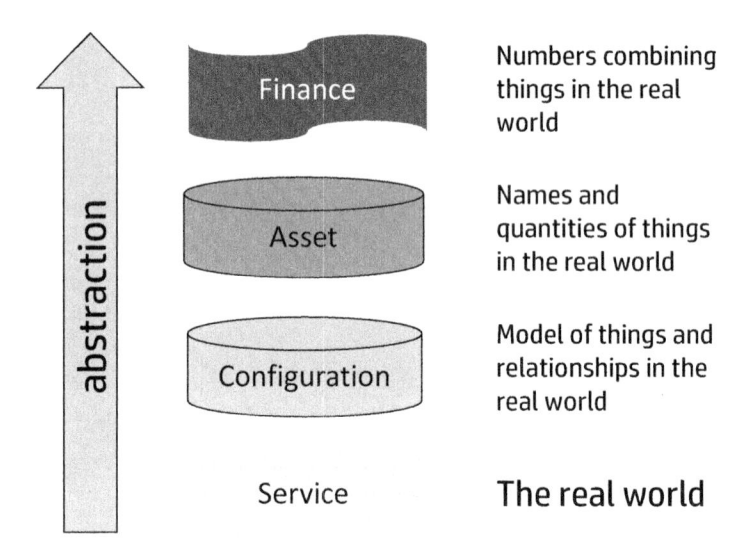

Figure 4.11 The abstraction relationship of the know-how resource type

There is another relationship between these systems that relates to the organisational structure and increasingly abstracted levels of interest at higher levels of management. This is shown in Figure 4.11. The real world of *operations* is first abstracted to a configuration which provides a detailed and accurate description of the things and their relationships in a system – including the user. This is next simplified to a list of assets and then finally to the quantities of assets transformed into financial values.

At each level, the same processes manage these systems and broadly can be described in the diagram shown in Figure 4.12 – without going too far into details. To distinguish it we will call this the repository lifecycle diagram.

All these processes are found at the real-world operational service level – often as very substantial ITIL processes in their own right. However, they also all exist in configuration management and asset management as sub processes to maintain the data records, and they all exist in financial management to maintain the detailed financial records. Parts of this representation have a strong resemblance to the operational loops of Chapter 1.

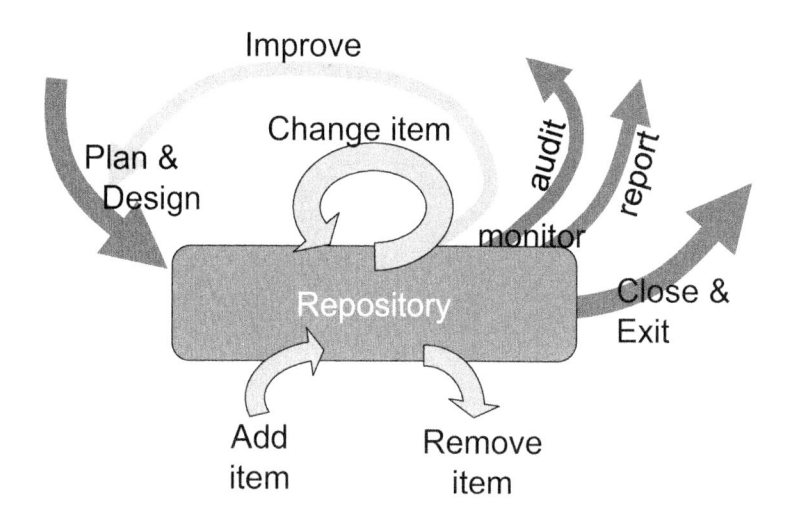

Figure 4.12 The generic lifecycle diagram for a repository

One of the most significant challenges in implementing ITIL approaches in organisations is establishing clear ownership for assets, configuration and knowledge without either creating seemingly endless, onerous, bureaucratic overheads, or making dangerous assumptions which allow this ownership to 'disappear down the cracks'.

Summary of processes mainly found in management

These seven processes – capacity management, availability management, service level management, information security management, configuration and asset management and knowledge management – four from Service Design and three from Service Transition – seem to be the only *management* processes operating *mainly* at the service level of an IT Service Management organisation.

Reframing ITIL

Coordination – aligning the services

Only one process fits mainly into the organisational system we have called *coordination* at the service level of the organisation:

Change management (and change evaluation)

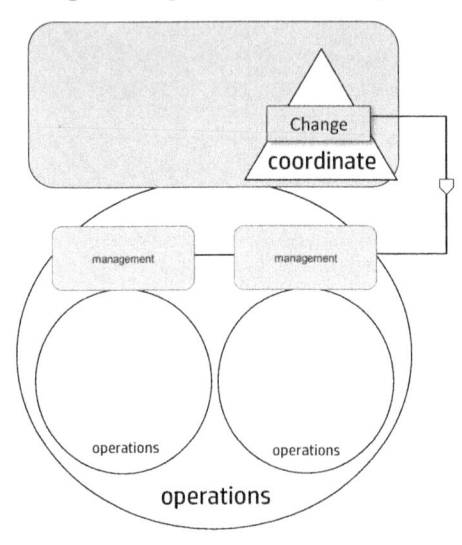

Figure 4.13 Change management mapped onto the *coordination* system

Change management [Service Transition] is a true process – or really a set of processes – and is one of the most important in ITIL. Despite its name, it is really about keeping change under control and is critical to protect both infrastructure and services from unauthorised change.

In particular, change management ensures that a change cannot be made to a service by one part of the organisation without effective planning and assessment, or the other parts being taken into account and/or informed. With such a complicated, interlocking system as IT, often with a relationship between parts over several different technologies, locations, or regions, this is essential to prevent chaos.

Examples of change advisory boards (CABs)

Organisational CABs maintain oversight and control of physical and software engineering, within or across several technology platforms.

CABs run for or by customers, where multiple organisations may be required to peer review, assess, approve and schedule changes across a complex web of physical and application platforms.

Change evaluation is called upon to evaluate significant changes, such as a substantial change to an existing service or introduction of a new service. The process is used to validate decisions taken regarding proposed changes.

As a set of coordination processes, change management has aspects that are suitable to small, frequent, fairly standard changes and to larger, less frequent, often custom changes.

For standard changes, change management frequently makes use of a 'pre-authorised change' system especially for use when incidents are fixed and sometimes when some requests are fulfilled. For larger, custom changes, change management uses the change advisory board (CAB) system. These two types of system – automation and standards on the one side and coordinating meetings on the other – are frequently both found in *coordination*.

As regards the resource types that are addressed by change in ITIL, change is almost entirely concerned with specialist IT infrastructure, both physical and virtual (i.e. applications), and occasionally facilities. The same processes could be applied to people, know-how and all facilities, but usually are not. A consequence of this can be that resources (people) able to resolve problems or design systems are allowed to depart to pastures new without adequate transition/replacement planning – resulting in panic when they are needed and missed, often long delays and a poor quality service.

A further limitation on the effectiveness of change management is that it is nearly always exclusively applied in the support department(s) – and not during the course of development projects. It is perhaps, reasonably, assumed that projects have their own change processes. Unfortunately this can occasionally prove to be something of a rash assumption.

The whole picture

So far we have looked at how each process contributes to, and fits into, the management systems of a service. It is equally useful to look at this from the perspective of the total service management system to see how complete it is (*operations* is not included). This is shown in Figure 4.14, and although it looks as though most of the management systems are covered, there is no provision for people and capabilities within any of the processes. *Innovation* is also only provided within the specialist processes indicated.

To make service management work as an organisation it is necessary to include four of the processes that are principally managed at the service organisation level (see Chapter 5) and which also have substantial components here at the service level. These are added as grey, italic boxes at the bottom in Figure 4.15. They are financial management, business relationship management, supplier management and demand management. There is no problem in doing this as all of these are designed to apply at the service level of the organisation as well as at the service organisation level – see Figure 5.3. The full set of

Reframing ITIL

these processes is also shown in Table 4.1 so that the components can be seen more clearly.

| | Manage ||| Coordinate | Innovate |
	resource	requirements	performance		
Capacity		specialist & facilities			
Availability		specialist & facilities			
Service Level					
Information Security					
Asset					
Configuration		information			
Knowledge		information			
Change					
Financial					
Business Relationship					
Supplier		people & capabilities			
Demand					

Table 4.1 Organisational systems described by the ITIL processes managing the service

It is worth commenting again that it is not uncommon for only a subset of these processes to be implemented in a given IT support organisation and this inevitably reduces the 'roundedness' of the organisational systems.

Resourcing staff

Even with these four extra processes added, people and capabilities are not explicitly resourced except through supplier management (see Chapter 5) – when the resource is provided by third parties. There is a real risk that those processes that generate requirements – such as capacity, availability, service level and security management – but which do not themselves provide financial resource, are not sufficiently integrated with financial management to ensure that sufficient resource would be made available to meet these requirements. One also shouldn't forget the needs of the *operations* processes in development (Figure 3.14) and support (Figure 2.14) for financial resource. Again the full (financial) resource negotiation loop needs to be integrated with these processes in service management.

Chapter 4 – Managing the Service

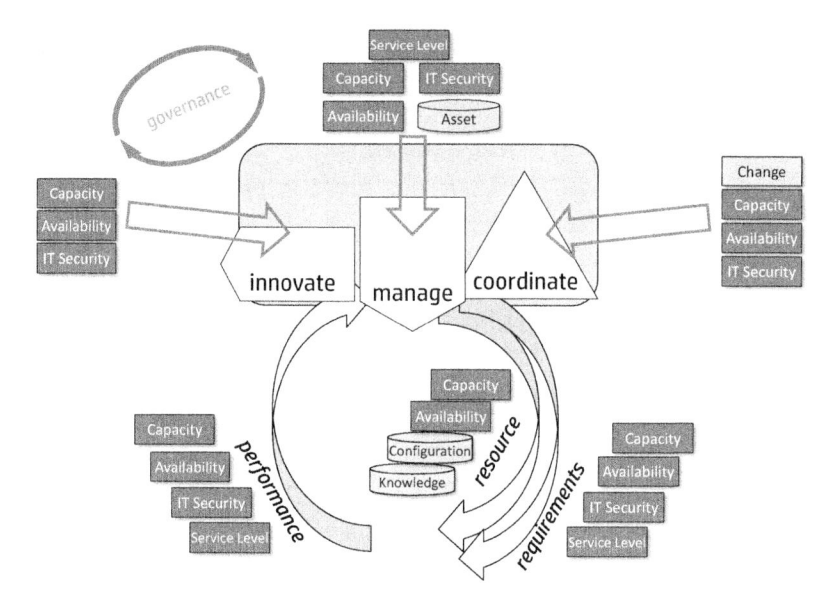

Figure 4.14 "Managing the service" processes mapped onto the organisational model showing all the management systems

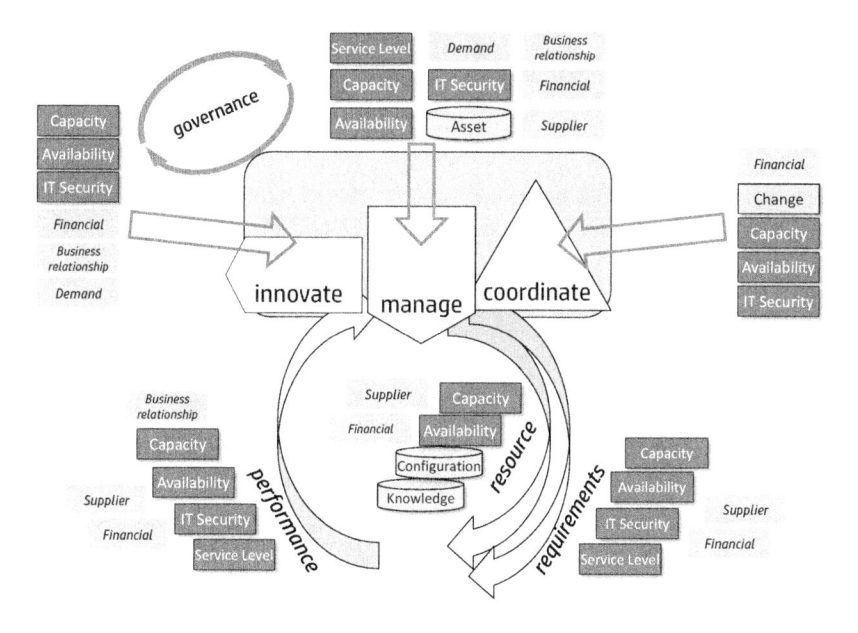

Figure 4.15 "Managing the service" processes mapped onto the organisational model including three extra processes from the next organisational level

77

Financial management may be deemed to provide general people and capabilities resource indirectly. However, this is complicated by the divorce of capability needs (usually mediated by an HR department) from financial planning in many situations. And, although service levels have a people element, requirements and performance for the people and capabilities resources are not provided or monitored through this. One consequence of this lack of integration is that divorcing the pressures to perform from the provision of resource produces severely stressed staff and management.

To compound this, change management is also rarely applied to people and capabilities: Although any competent business would be expected to have continuity and succession plans for staff, it is remarkably common for this not to be the case. The absence of this as an element of ITIL 3, which aspires to be a full model in its current iterations, either at this service level or the service organisation level does not encourage this good behaviour. Applying demand and change management to people could greatly improve IT support management – as could enlarging the scope of knowledge management to include culture and behaviours. In ITIL 4 the workforce and talent management practice remedies this omission.

Chapter 5

Managing the Service Organisation

In this chapter we are going to follow the same approach as in Chapter 4 to look at ITIL processes that are part of the management of the service organisation (the level above service) – the IT department or account.

The ITIL frame

As we look at the remaining ITIL processes – those we haven't already covered – we are working on upwards into the organisation. We judge these processes to be more relevantly applied at the next level up from the service – a level we have called the service organisation – see Figure 5.3. Some also impact back down the management chain into lower levels. In an in-house IT environment the service organisation would be the IT department. In an outsourced IT environment this would be the IT account.

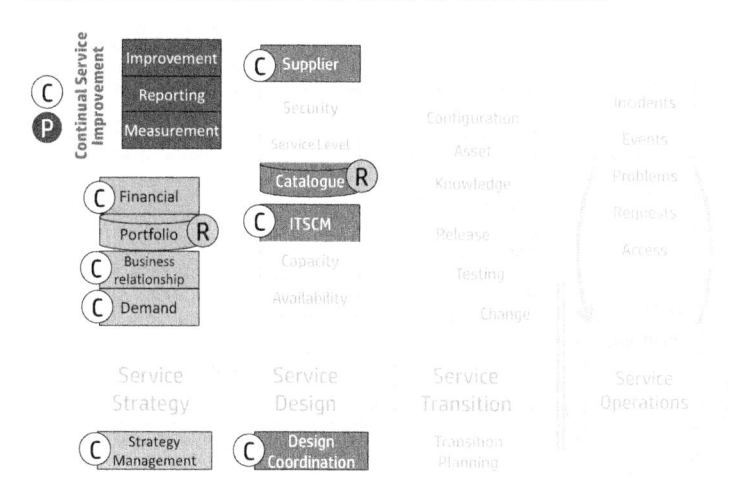

Figure 5.1 ITIL 'processes' considered in Chapter 5.
C = capability; R = repository

79

Reframing ITIL

The processes under discussion are shown in Figure 5.1 and come from the ITIL 3 Service Strategy, Service Design and Continual Service Improvement disciplines. Although some contain processes, they are more correctly considered to be either capabilities or repositories.

ITIL 'processes' by management system

The same management systems as described in the last chapter are relevant – however here, they describe the higher organisational level and the two structures in *operations* in Figure 5.2 represent two services which are each equivalent to the higher level in Chapter 4. We can do this because the organisational model we are using is recursive – i.e. each level fits into the layer above as both have the same underlying structure.

The four resource types introduced in Chapter 4 are still relevant here and will be considered as they arise.

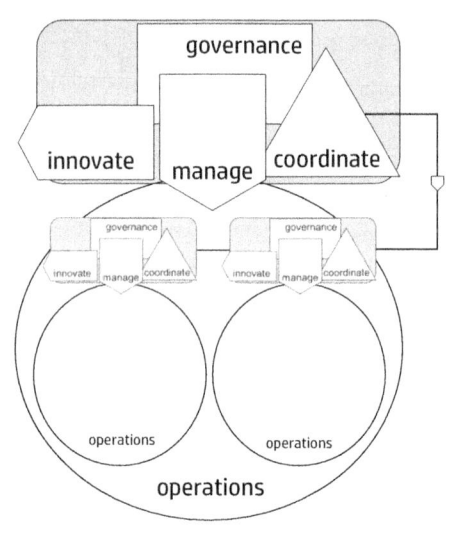

Figure 5.2 Detail of management processes at the service organisation level

The scope of the 'processes' described here are shown in summary in Figure 5.3. We have brought them together as being involved in 'managing the service organisation' where most of them actually sit, for ease of discussion. It may be seen that the scope of the management of some processes also occurs at other levels of the organisation as indicated by the arrows and vertical position of the process boxes.

The Figure shows four layers of recursion – i.e. four levels of the organisation – together. This makes it possible to indicate the levels of the organisation that each process (broadly) covers – the arrows indicate the spread of coverage.

Service Design as a process was discussed in Chapter 3 but is included in this diagram to show how it encompasses the different levels of the organisation.

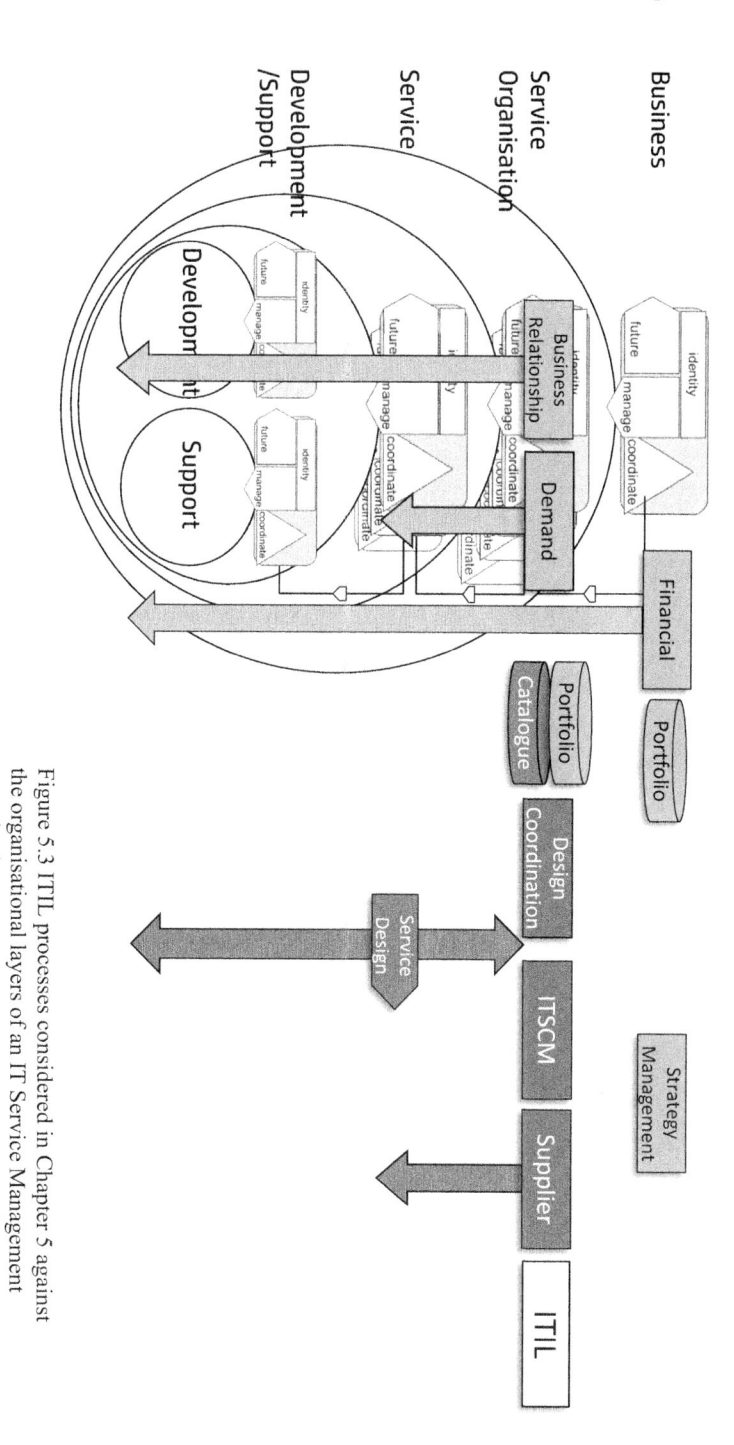

Chapter 5 – Managing the Service Organisation

Figure 5.3 ITIL processes considered in Chapter 5 against the organisational layers of an IT Service Management organisation

81

Management – the resource negotiation loop

As with our discussion of 'Managing the Service' in Chapter 4, the following processes contain mostly activities that fit into the system we have called *management* and which encompasses the resource negotiation loop:

Financial management

Financial management [Service Strategy] is a true set of processes as well as being a capability. It is one of three processes discussed in this chapter which actually belongs elsewhere, namely at the even higher organisational level of the whole business (Figure 5.3). It is debatable whether ITIL should be advising a business how to run its finances – even the finances of the IT department – as the relevant processes, standards and protocols will already be in place for any existing business.

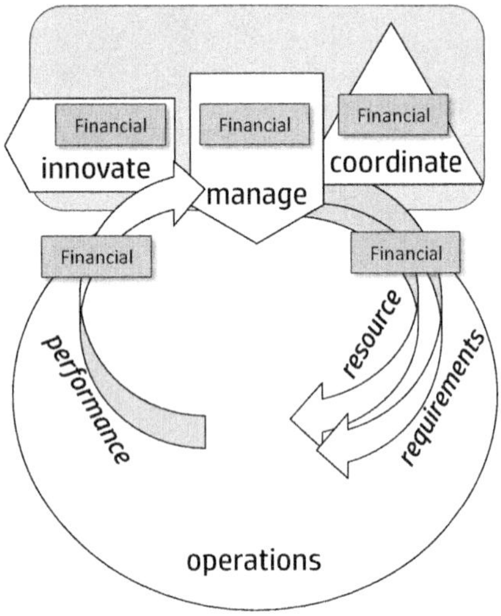

Figure 5.4 Financial management mapped onto the *management* resource negotiation loop

In Figure 5.4, the rectangular, grey *management* box here represents the whole business management department (see also Figure 5.3) and *operations* represents the rest of the business, including the IT department – remember that this is a recursive model. It might be assumed that, as this version of financial management is defined by ITIL, the processes as described only apply to the IT department – but see the comments already made about the appropriateness of this.

Financial management is the main process that can control allocation of financial resource, the financial requirements and financial performance monitoring. Hence it is a fully rounded *management* process. To do any of this effectively, it must be fully integrated with all the other management processes. Sadly, this is rarely the case and problems ensue.

Financial management also has an important component in the *innovation* system which interacts with the *management* system to provide financial forecasts. Another important component is present as the standards that

Chapter 5 – Managing the Service Organisation

financial management provides through the *coordination* system at the top level. This ensures that the whole organisation operates to the same standards and follows the same processes in consolidating financial data for consideration at each level and for the highest level. This is a no-brainer but is, incredibly, not always followed in IT organisations where different departments can use different packages and standards in managing their finances at lower levels in the organisation. So overall, this is a well-rounded set of processes as would be expected for finance.

Although our discussion has been about financial management at the highest level in the organisation – these processes should also be found at all levels in the IT organisation for it to work effectively. This is a case where the processes should be in use at all recursive levels, driven from the top.

Catalogue and portfolio management

Catalogue management [Service Design] and portfolio management [Service Strategy] are closely related and so will be discussed together from an organisational perspective. Both are active principally at the service organisation (IT outsource account / IT Department) level, although portfolio management may also operate at the whole business level (Figure 5.3).

Both are shown in the ITIL framing diagram (Figure 5.1) as repositories – that is, they hold descriptions of real or potential things – specifically services.

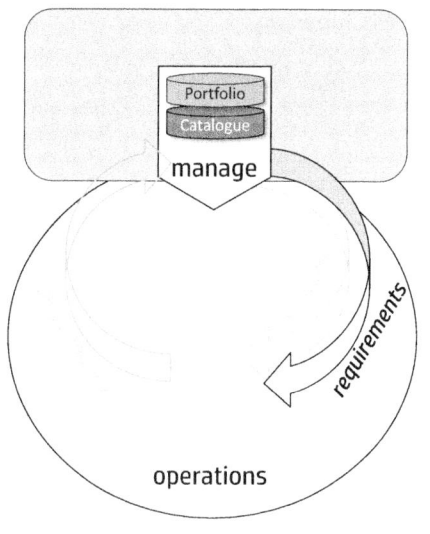

Figure 5.5 Catalogue and portfolio management mapped onto the *management* resource negotiation loop

The service portfolio holds descriptions of all the services that an IT outsourcer (or, less relevantly, an IT department) offers and might offer and may be held at the level above service organisation in an outsource provider. These descriptions are used to help in making strategic decisions regarding customer interest and motivation, pricing, strengths and weaknesses, resource allocation and value realisation.

Reframing ITIL

Portfolio management describes a set of processes that manage the whole lifecycle of the service portfolio (Figure 5.5). This includes providing mechanisms for the planning the service lifecycles – including looking for new services, planning and resourcing their development, evaluating their strategic value, their provision and their termination.

It is possible to take the generic lifecycle diagram introduced in Chapter 4 (Figure 4.11) and see that it also applies to the portfolio management lifecycle (Figure 5.6). Indeed, it applies to all repositories which are, in essence, abstractions of the real world.

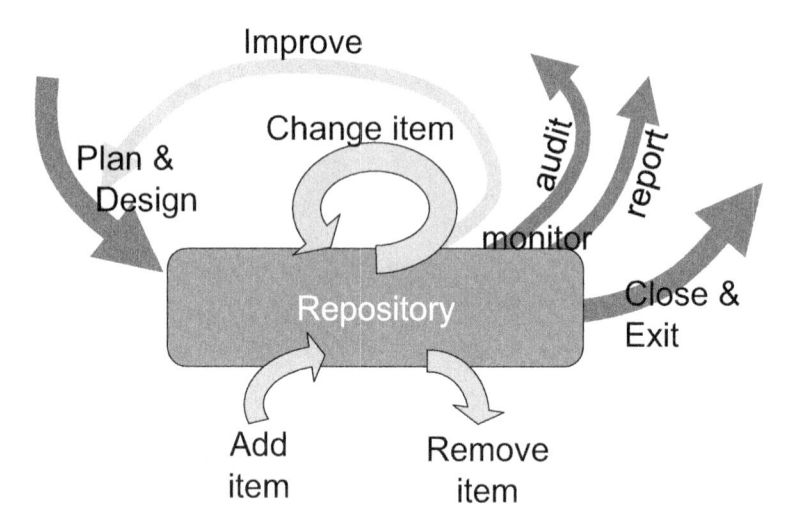

Figure 5.6 The generic lifecycle management diagram for repositories

So, staying with an IT outsourcer, if the service portfolio defines the services that *can* be offered by any account to any (potential) client from a business perspective – the service catalogue is a more detailed description of a subset of services – the operational services – that *are* being used by an account to support a particular client. Clearly there must therefore be a separate service catalogue for each client.

As with portfolio, catalogue management is a set of processes that manage the lifecycle of the service catalogues (Figure 5.5). Again the lifecycle management diagram is applicable (Figure 5.6).

For each client there should be two views of the service catalogue: a business service catalogue providing a view outward to the client and a technical service catalogue providing a view down and inward to the delivery organisation.

Chapter 5 – Managing the Service Organisation

It is worth adding that the service catalogue can have a recursive structure – looking upwards with services grouped together into service packages which are provided together or are technically integrated (client or technical view); looking downwards into lower-level services which together constitute a service. In fact, the relationship can be more of a network than recursive in some cases. In this sense, the service catalogue can have a (much) higher level resemblance to the configuration management system.

It is important to note that catalogue management is *not* concerned with the online catalogue that is frequently offered to the users for making standard requests. This confusion is very common and some IT suppliers try, incorrectly, to use catalogue management for this purpose.

Supplier management

Supplier management [Service Design] is a capability that includes all the processes for managing suppliers. The processes are concerned with the provision of financial resource to the supplier to allow them to deliver a given performance against defined requirements. These would normally be defined in a contract between the IT service organisation and the supplier.

In Figure 5.7 the *operations* blob represents a supplier – in this case the work is done by a department which is actually part of the supplier organisation. The supplier organisation may deliver a whole service to the service organisation or a part of a service at a slightly lower level in the organisation. Management of the relationship by supplier management is the same in both cases although one may be carried out at the service organisation level and the other at the service level.

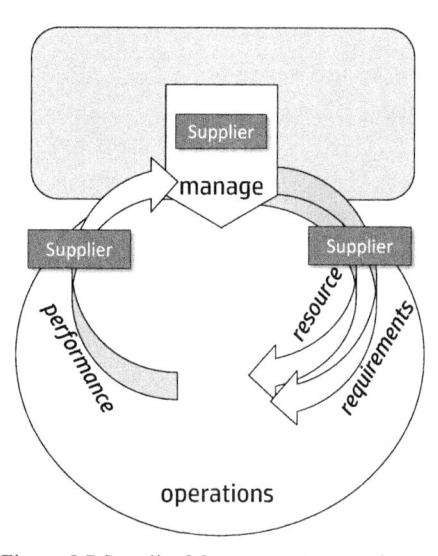

Figure 5.7 Supplier Management mapped onto the *management* resource negotiation loop

Reframing ITIL

The supplier management capability provides a rounded set of *management* processes that ensures the supplier is delivering effectively to the service organisation or service.

ITSCM

IT service continuity management [Service Design] is distantly related to availability management in that it is concerned with the availability exception: when service availability drops to zero and needs to be recovered. ITSCM supports the business continuity management process.

ITSCM is a capability that details how the business operates under these zero-availability conditions and how the services are recovered and restored. A set of ITSCM plans are produced and maintained for this eventuality.

There is a more direct intervention into *operations* through providing requirements that ensure that risk is managed at an agreed level. In support of this there are exercises to ensure plans are being kept up to date (the performance half-loop). The requirements and performance aspects of ITSCM are balances, but there is no resource provision or management thereof as a part of ITSCM as shown in Figure 5.8.

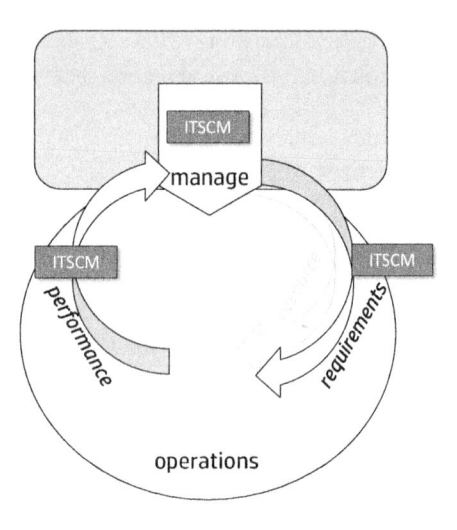

Figure 5.8 IT Service Continuity Management mapped onto the *management* resource negotiation loop

Other *management* activities include providing a centre of expertise, assessing the impact of changes and making input to supplier management.

Design coordination

Design coordination [Service Design] is a full management capability. The *coordination* purpose of design coordination is suggested by the name, but many of the activities and processes within it lie in the resource negotiation loop of *management* – hence its inclusion in this section (Figure 5.9).

86

Chapter 5 – Managing the Service Organisation

Design coordination has a role in resource allocation by planning and coordinating the resources required to design services.

It has roles in providing requirements through producing service design packages (SDPs), and managing their progress into Service Transition; managing quality criteria and ensuring all models and solutions correspond to corporate requirements.

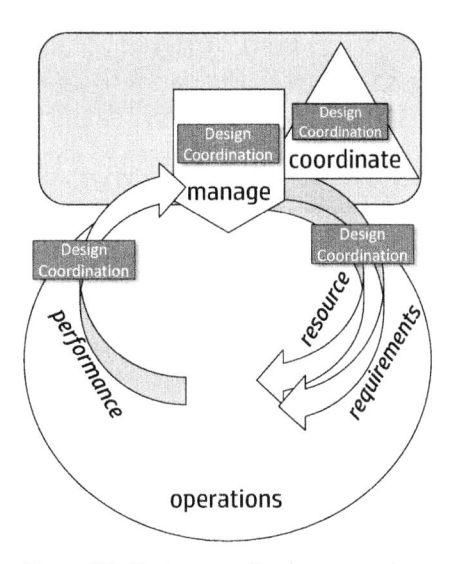

Figure 5.9 Design coordination mapped onto the *management* resource negotiation loop

Finally it monitors performance of the whole service design lifecycle stage and hence it manages a fully rounded set of *management* processes that ensure services are effectively designed.

There is also a *coordination* role in ensuring that all parties adopt a common set of practices and systems where appropriate. A further role in this space is the management of schedules and conflicts between design projects.

Continual service improvement

Although continual service improvement (CSI) is not described as a process, the one process it does describe – the seven-step improvement process – is more of a methodology for improvement than an IT process. It is more appropriate, therefore, to consider CSI as an approach in itself – see Figure 5.10.

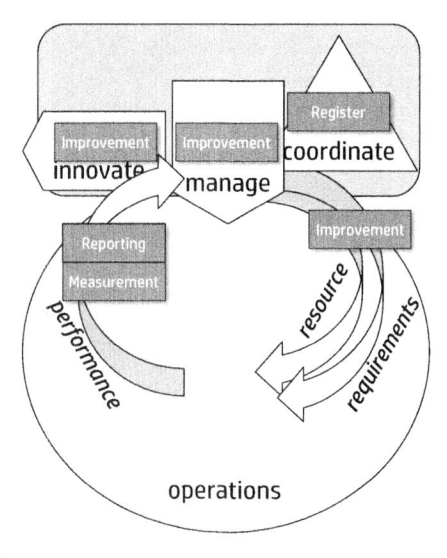

Figure 5.10 Continual service improvement mapped onto the *management* resource negotiation loop

87

Although CSI contains the word improvement, many of the components described are more strongly associated with *management* than *innovation*: monitoring, service levels and change are all *management* components.

A significant CSI role is to gather together recommendations for improvement activities. In deference to this and the inclusion of some (incremental) improvement methodologies in CSI, the association with *innovation* is shown in the diagram.

CSI has a role in management through its control of the improvement register and a role in resource allocation by planning and coordinating the resources required to improve services through projects. It also has roles in the provision of requirements by defining the improvements required.

Finally it monitors performance of the improvements through reporting and measurement and hence it manages a fully rounded set of *management* processes that ensure services are improved.

CSI also has a significant role in *coordination* through ownership, control and maintenance of the improvement register which ensure that 'improvement projects' are prioritised and managed centrally.

CSI is normally managed at the account level (or the IT department level if IT is in-house), but some aspects may be more effectively operated at the IT service level.

Summary of management processes
These seven processes – catalogue, supplier and IT service continuity management and design coordination from Service Design; financial and portfolio management from Service Strategy, and several from Continual Service Improvement – are the main *management* processes operating principally at the service organisation level (and above) of an IT service management organisation.

Innovation – preparing the service organisation for the future
Although a number of the processes introduced in the *management* section above have *innovation* components, for demand management, described here, it is the main purpose of its existence. For business relationship management, *innovation* is dominant but *management* is also important.

Chapter 5 – Managing the Service Organisation

Demand management

The demand management process [Service Strategy] is a capability that is intended to assess the demand for future resource resulting from new requests and developments. This occurs mainly at the service organisation level (IT client account level if outsourced, IT department if support is in-house). Occasionally there are also demand management activities at the lower, service level.

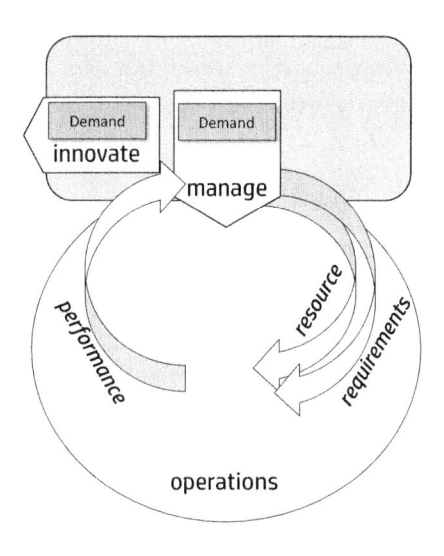

Figure 5.11 Demand management mapped onto the *innovation* system

To do this its processes sit in *innovation* in order to identify future requirements as well as in *management* to look into the organisation to assess existing resource at all levels and plan the response for new demand – the performance and resource parts of the loop respectively.

Business relationship management

The business relationship management process [Service Strategy] is a capability that is intended to manage a constructive relationship between a service provider and client. The focus is usually both strategic and tactical and so sits at the service organisation level but reaches down to the service level and even below.

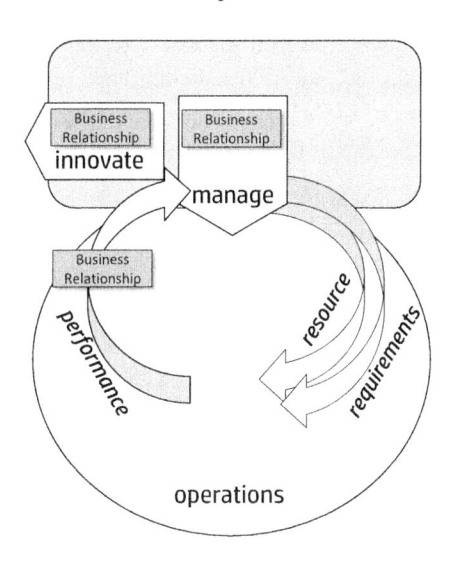

Figure 5.12 Business relationship management mapped onto the *innovation* system

To do this its processes sit in *innovation* in order to effectively communicate out to the client and also in *management* to look into the organisation to ensure that it is

89

delivering effectively on the client's requirements (Figure 5.12).

Coordination – aligning the service organisation

ITIL

ITIL of itself has a significant role in providing standards that all the departments of the service organisation must follow.

ITIL is usually owned and managed at the top, outsourced service supplier level. In large accounts it may be owned by the client accounts. Where support is in-house it is owned by the IT department.

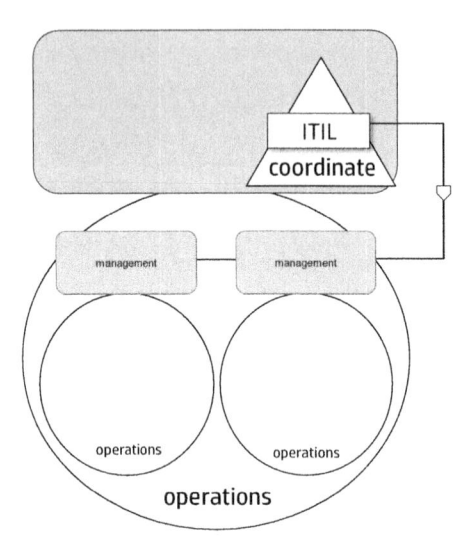

Figure 5.13 ITIL mapped onto the *coordination* system

The department that is responsible for doing this is normally known as IT Service Management (ITSM) or something similar. There is also some active management of the processes from this department in terms of providing requirements and monitoring performance – not shown here. *Coordination* passes the standards down through the organisation to all the underlying levels (Figure 5.13).

In some cases, perhaps because historically ITIL 2 was seen to be focused mainly on service support (using the terminology used in this book) rather than service development, the IT Service Management department may be found in the service support organisation of one of the major services of an account. This is perhaps done unconsciously because ITIL is still seen as mainly operational and of less importance than other non-IT business management processes.

Where this is the case, it provides the challenge of getting other services to follow the same standards – as well as service development. Even more difficult is the challenge of getting higher levels of the IT organisation to adopt the ITIL approaches.

Chapter 5 – Managing the Service Organisation

Governance – balancing innovation and management

Although strategy management for IT services has a strong *innovation* role, its context of balancing this against the existing business, sits it principally in *governance*.

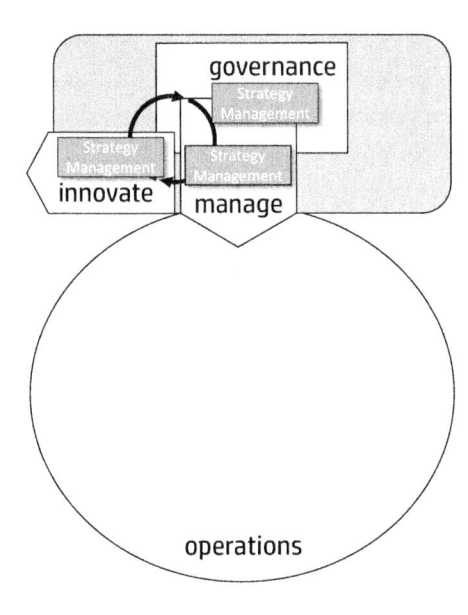

Figure 5.14 Strategy management for IT services mapped onto the *governance* system

Strategy management for IT services

The strategy management process [Service Strategy] is a capability that is intended to assess and identify opportunities internal and external to the service provider. This occurs mainly at the service provider level and so is different from a number of other processes in focusing on the service provider rather than the client business. However, it is possible to see a role for it in in-house IT provision. It is also at a level above the service organisation and so, referring back to the diagram in Figure 5.2, *operations* represent a number of client accounts.

Because it is outward looking and future facing, strategy management has a presence in *innovation*. However its role in translating strategic plans into tactical and operational plans sits firmly in *management*. Overall the focus is strategic and so strategy management has a key role in balancing the *governance* loop (Figure 5.14).

The whole picture for the service organisation

So far we have looked at how each process contributes to and fits into the management systems of the IT organisation. It is equally useful to look at this from the perspective of the management system of the service organisation to see how complete it is.

Reframing ITIL

In Figure 5.15 we have slightly simplified the management diagram to include the components that we have been discussing above. As before, the key management systems are shown as *innovate (= innovation)* – looking to the future; *coordinate (=coordination)* – keeping activities aligned; and *manage (=management)* – which ensures enough resources are available and measures performance against the requirements. Also shown is the governance loop between *management* (focused on the present) and *innovation* (focused on the future) although the governance block is not explicitly included. See also Table 5.1 below for an alternative view.

On the face of it this looks like a fairly healthy and balanced set of processes. Note that service level management is also included here (as part of *management*), although mainly focused on managing the service (Chapter 4).

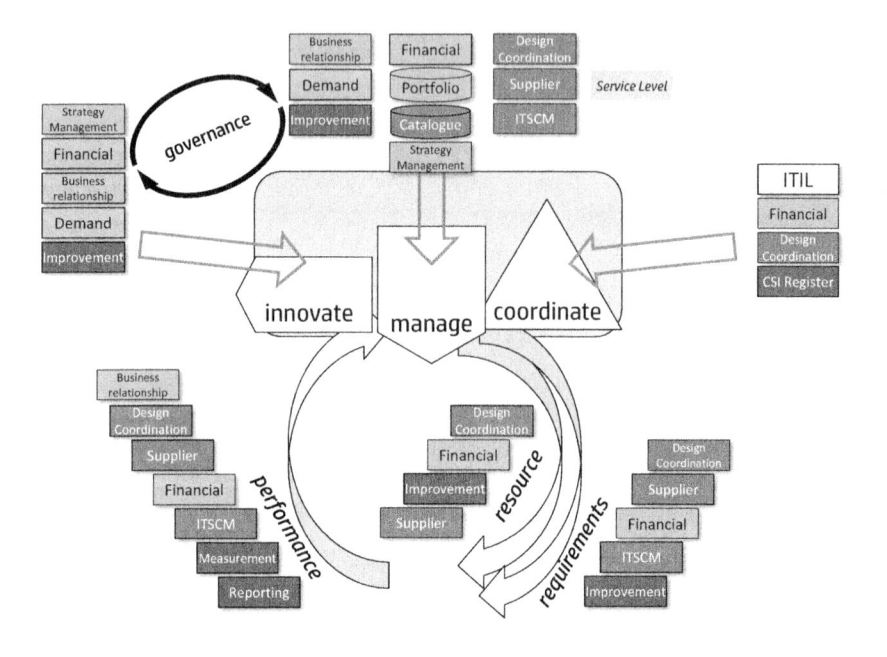

Figure 5.15 "Managing the service organisation" processes mapped onto the organisational model showing all the systems

Perhaps the biggest problem is that although tightly defining the processes, ITIL 3 doesn't adequately encourage their integration together and into the general organisation. It remains to be seen whether ITIL 4 is more successful in this. Managing the processes and their integration as part of the management of the organisation is key, but ITIL is frequently seen as 'separate' from general management and, at the best, informs it but isn't actively involved. The owners of the ITIL processes are often relatively junior staff and are not given very much voice in managing the organisation.

This shouldn't be a surprise. What organisation with any pretensions would use a framework like ITIL to manage its financial system, its strategy, its business relationships – regardless of how good the recommendations might be?

This is where it all falls apart: If ITIL were actually used flexibly as the template for managing the organisation, it could – at least in principle – do so quite effectively. However, when ITIL is adopted piecemeal – and it always is – and usually as a bolt-on to the pre-existing general management of the IT service organisation, it fails to provide an integrated management system. The weakest part of ITIL, as implemented but perhaps not as intended, is its integration.

| | Manage ||| Coordinate | Innovate |
	resource	requirements	performance		
Financial					
Strategy Management					
Business Relationship					
Demand					
Portfolio					
Catalogue					
Supplier		people & capabilities			
ITSCM					
Design Coordination					
CSI	improvement	improvement	improvement	reporting measurement	register	improvement
ITIL					
Service Level					

Table 5.1 Organisational systems described by the ITIL processes managing the service organisation (*governance* not included)

Another area of weakness here is in the tempo of each of the processes. To be effective, they need to feed into each other as and when required. In reality, partly because they are so disconnected, they beat their own drums and work to their own timetables in an uncoordinated way. Hence feedback, budgets etc.. from a specific area are not available when required and special 'hares' are often set running to collect statistics (performance) or provide funding (resource), with the inevitable disruption and waste of effort this entails. A major side effect of this is the stress caused to staff and managers who are trying to deliver with inadequate or inappropriate resource.

Perhaps the biggest area of weakness for the long-term survival of a given IT support organisation is the weakness in the transformative improvement arena in ITIL. This should be part of *innovation* but is largely missing; one might expect it to be the domain of Continual Service Improvement but this generally deals with much smaller issues. For minor improvements problem management, where implemented, can be most effective.

Finally, the lack of integration and incompleteness (of management processes) of many IT organisations does not mean that they cannot exist and prosper. Indeed, many such organisations do, and do. It is when challenges occur – and they always do – that their weaknesses emerge in an inability to respond adequately without generating what can often be a downward spiral of organisational implosion. More complete and rounded organisations do not do this – this is what is meant by an organisation's viability. Hence the name 'viable system model'.

Chapter 6

Designing the Service Organisation

– organisational issues of the first kind

In this chapter we look into how services are most effectively delivered in various shapes of organisation, and to do this it is necessary to first take a quick diversion into representing organisations. This will allow us to systematically discuss the alternatives for IT departments or accounts.

The ITIL 3 disciplines do each consider organisational design from their various perspectives. It is worth a look at these but please bear in mind that the points below apply whichever of these is considered. Note that so-called matrix organisations, which are often advocated, pretty much invariably have one *management* dimension – where resource is provided – and one or more *coordination* dimensions. To identify the *management* dimension, look for the funding.

The 'blob' frame

The diagram in Figure 6.1 shows a whole organisation with departments, groups, sections, teams identified by circles all nested within each other. It is fairly intuitive that a smaller circle is a unit that is organisationally within a larger unit etc... Although intuitive, it is quite difficult to use this diagram when discussing the specifics of an organisation, so we use a shorthand version, as in

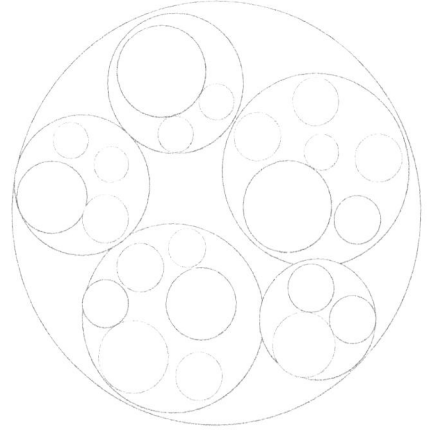

Figure 6.1 Organisational diagram showing nested organisational units

Figure 6.2, which we will call the blob diagram. In this case, the focus is on the bottom right hand unit of Figure 6.1 with three smaller units. This is the organisational representation we will use in this chapter. It looks a bit like a hierarchy diagram, but is focused on the organisational units rather than individual roles.

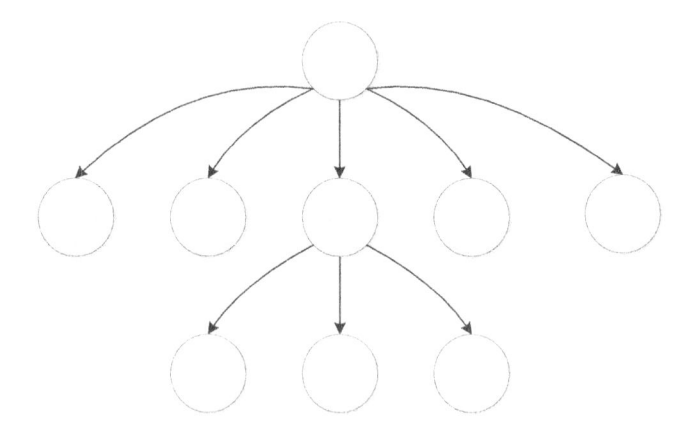

Figure 6.2 Organisational representation showing organisational units in a 'blob' diagram

The classic/simplified IT organisation

So far in this discussion, we have presented an organisation that has the IT layers below the 'client' business (whether that be a parent business or an outsourcer) consisting of the IT department (the service organisation), services, and then a breakdown into development/support and finally the operational processes – Figure 6.3. These are logical from a delivery perspective but do not fully represent the complexity of a real IT organisation.

There is likely to be a project office and an ITSM department at the senior level to ensure that all the projects in the development groups and the processes in the support groups follow agreed standards. To represent these, we use the triangles previously introduced for *coordination*.

This particular simple organisation is nice and logical but could not completely represent real IT service organisations as it does not directly and explicitly include the additional dimensions of technology or customer. In fact, very few IT delivery organisations actually look like Figure 6.3

Chapter 6 – Designing the Service Organisation

Note that there are also many occasions where the actual organisation – as identified by seeing what actually happens and who has control of resource – differs from the organisation as drawn on the organisation's hierarchy chart. In that event, it is always important to work with the actual organisational structure.

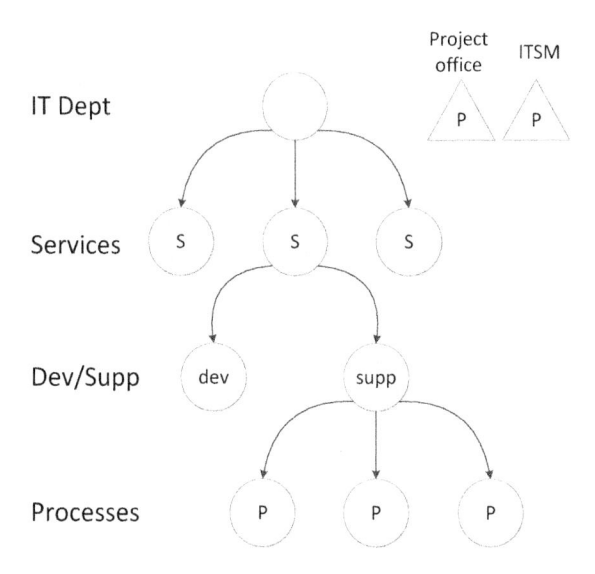

Figure 6.3 Blob diagram of the classic/simplified IT organisation

In search of the ideal IT department

The most useful way to approach this is to pose a series of theoretical organisational possibilities and then discuss the advantages and disadvantages of each. These are still considerably simplified in comparison to real organisations, but allow principles to be established and consequences explained.

More reality will then be introduced in the form of some example organisational types, and these will be presented with their advantages and disadvantages. It will be obvious at the end of this that there is no perfect solution, but the options will be on the table for informed decisions based on a systematic (and systemic) organisational approach.

Of the three widespread types of IT support organisation: namely 1) In-house; 2) Large outsourced account; and 3) Small outsourced account; the matrix we

Reframing ITIL

are going to use applies to 1) and 2). The different issues that occur with multiple small accounts managed by an outsourcer centrally will be discussed briefly in Chapter 7 – it is in this context that customer as an organisational dimension becomes most important.

To ensure this discussion is robust, we will use an organisational criteria matrix. This is an approach which may seem cumbersome, but which will prove to be capable of dealing with the many complex issues in comparing alternative organisations for IT support.

An organisational criteria matrix

In the process of developing this assessment, a matrix was produced of each organisational option assessed against a set of organisational criteria. This approach can be used for other types of organisation (than IT) with appropriate changes to the criteria. This matrix is shown in Table 6.6 and each assessment was given on a four point extended RAYG scale (see end of chapter for explanation) presented as red, amber, yellow, or green. We developed five criteria to use for this assessment. These were reduced from an initial ten which were then combined as the factors affecting them were seen to be almost the same and where there was also a logical reason to do so:

1. **END USER FOCUS (individual users)**
   Ability to absorb the complexity of demand
   - How well do the teams handle the work coming into the organisation?

2. Responsiveness to end-user needs (end-user focus on process and services)
   - How responsive is the organisation to the end user?

   Separate low/high volume and complexity activities
   - How well can routine, high volume activities be separated from complex, low volume activities?

3. **CLIENT FOCUS (the business client)**
   Strategic view – big change possible? (responsiveness to owners)
   - How responsive is the organisation to the client's requirements?

Coherence of a service to the client
- How coherently is a service managed from the client's perspective?

4. **RESOURCE FOCUS (staff and expertise)**
   Critical resource retention
   - How effectively does the organisation retain critical staff and expertise?

   Resource flexibility
   - Can resources easily move to other work to ensure they are not under (or over) utilised?

   Resource used efficiently

5. **KNOWLEDGE FOCUS**
   Knowledge generation and retention
   - How effectively does the organisational structure encourage knowledge generation and retention?

6. **DEVELOPMENT FOCUS (service development)**
   Continuity and quality of development and hand over to live
   - How good is development from a support perspective?
   - How effective is handover from one stage to the next?

These are not entirely independent but where there was significant dependence, the criteria have been merged. This is a complex piece of work and thirteen different organisational options – representing different orderings of service lines, ITIL processes, development/support and technology – were considered against these five criteria. Customer was not considered as part of the matrix although they are often synonymous or at least closely related to service lines. The focus is on support rather than development.

Five Examples

Thirteen options were considered, each assigned a letter from A to L. Five options: A, D, H, J and L are described in more detail below as a representative sample. In this initial survey there is no service desk (this is added later). The whole matrix of 13 options can be found in Table 6.6.

You may like to jump straight to Table 6.6 on page 110 for context and then refer back to the five examples to see how they work in detail.

Reframing ITIL

Option A – in Table 6.6

See Figure 6.4. In our first organisational option the IT unit is split at the highest level between services – where this is done, they may be referred to as service lines. This may be services for different clients within the parent/client business – often application based; this may be services such as communications, networks, servers etc..

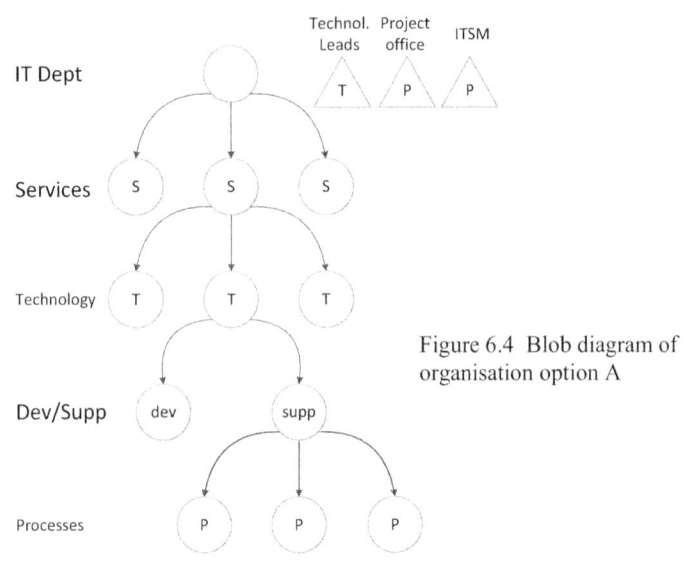

Figure 6.4 Blob diagram of organisation option A

Each service department is here broken down by the technologies used, keeping all the technology experts together in teams.

These teams are then split between development and support groups allowing for specialisation and often with a split between more experienced staff – development – and less experienced – support.

Within the support staff of a technology team, activities and perhaps even staff if the teams are large enough, are split between the various ITIL operations processes such as incident management, problem management, request fulfilment. Smaller groups or individuals would deal with the other processes.

There would probably be coordination of technologies at the highest level to ensure consistency between services. As ITIL processes sit at the bottom of the organisation, there would be an ITSM unit to ensure coordination of the IT service processes between all the service/technology-based support teams. A project office would probably also sit at a high level to provide support and

Chapter 6 – Designing the Service Organisation

ensure consistency between the projects operating in the various development teams.

So what are the issues with respect to the five criteria we have identified?

Table 6.1 RAYG assessment of organisation option A

RAYG	ISSUES
R	**1. END-USER FOCUS** With processes sitting at the lowest organisational level, end-user queries need to negotiate services and technologies before they find the correct process. End users rarely have the understanding to ensure this happens correctly. With process so low, this makes it virtually impossible to separate low/high volume and complex activities.
Y	**2. CLIENT FOCUS** The service is at a high level in the structure and so can be well represented to the client. However, development is split between technologies and the technology lead would need to coordinate technology issues in projects.
Y	**3. RESOURCE FOCUS** Resource is mainly technology constrained. However, a given resource cannot work on different services as they separate at the top. Resource can work on different processes which is good for efficiency. Although support resource could be moved to development, it is normally separate
G	**4. KNOWLEDGE FOCUS** Service knowledge can be effectively retained by the service teams and includes development and support knowledge. Technology knowledge is also at a high level. Process knowledge could be hard to retain.
G	**5. DEVELOPMENT FOCUS** Because technology teams sit under services, although split between development and support, it is relatively easy for these two activities to communicate or even share staff.

Reframing ITIL

Option D- in Table 6.6

In our next organisational option the development unit is managed separately at the top level and has a number of programmes and projects below it (not shown here). It would likely have a project office and service leads at the highest level.

The support department is split by the major operational ITIL processes such as incident management, problem management and request fulfilment.

Each process department is split into the major services, e.g. servers, networks, communications, and each of these may be split into technology teams or just have technology experts depending on the size of the operation.

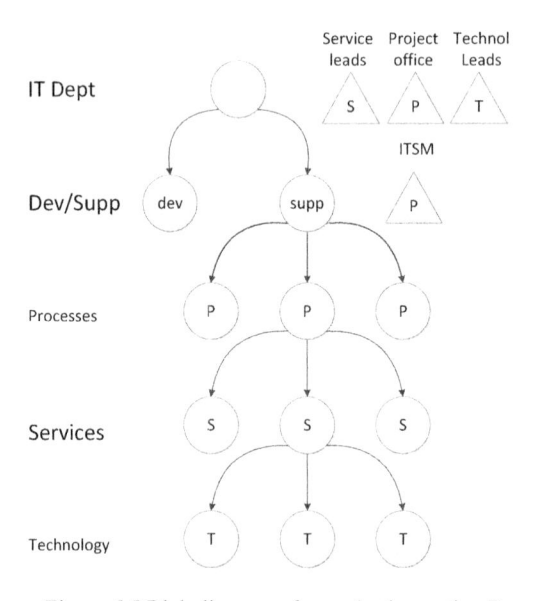

Figure 6.5 Blob diagram of organisation option D

Again, there would probably be coordination of the services at the highest level to ensure that development and support and the various processes are working in alignment. There would probably also be a coordination of technologies at the same level – or at the support department level – to ensure technologies are in alignment between development and support and between the various service support units. Although ITIL processes sit fairly high up in the organisation, there may still be an ITSM unit – perhaps at the support level – to

Chapter 6 – Designing the Service Organisation

ensure coordination of the other IT service processes between all the service/technology-based support teams.

So what are the issues with respect to the five criteria we have identified?

Table 6.2 RAYG assessment of organisation option D

RAYG	ISSUES
G	**1. END-USER FOCUS** The ITIL processes – such as incident management – own all the services and technologies and so can respond appropriately to any end-user enquiry. The same applies to the other operational processes. It also makes it easy to separate low/high volume and complex activities.
A	**2. CLIENT FOCUS** The service is at rather a low level in the support organisation, sitting below ITIL process and so is fragmented. Development is also separate and the service lead would be needed to coordinate process, development and support issues.
R	**3. RESOURCE FOCUS** Resource is mainly technology constrained. A given resource cannot work on different services or ITIL processes as they are in entirely different teams. Support resource also cannot work on development. Hence resource focus is very narrow and may not have enough interest for retention.
R	**4. KNOWLEDGE FOCUS** Service knowledge is separated by process. Knowledge from development is also separated. Technology knowledge is generated at the very bottom and in isolation within a process and service.
R	**5. DEVELOPMENT FOCUS** Because the whole organisation is split at the highest level into development and support, communication and handover between these two groups would be challenging.

Reframing ITIL

Option H– in Table 6.6

In our next organisational option the development unit is also managed separately at the top level and has a number of programmes and projects below it (not shown here). It would likely have a project office at the highest level and possibly technology leads.

The support department is split by major service, e.g. servers, networks, communications, and each of these by technology teams. Although not shown it is likely that the development department is also split by services.

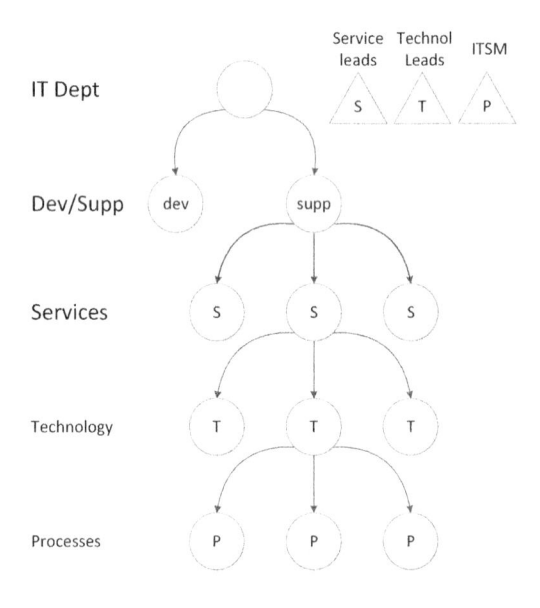

Figure 6.6 Blob diagram of organisation option H

All the technology teams carry out all the (relevant) IT processes such as incident management, problem management and request fulfilment.

There would probably be coordination of the services at the highest level to ensure that development and support are working in alignment. There would probably also be a coordination of technologies at the same level – or at the support department level – to ensure technologies are in alignment between development and support and between the various service support units.

Chapter 6 – Designing the Service Organisation

Finally there would be an ITSM unit to ensure coordination of the IT service processes between all the technology-based support teams.

So what are the issues with respect to the five criteria we have identified?

Table 6.3 RAYG assessment of organisation option H

RAYG	ISSUES
R	**1. END-USER FOCUS** With processes sitting at the lowest organisational level, the end user cannot get a sensible response to enquiries, as they first need to negotiate services and technologies. Complexity and volume management are process issues. As these are carried out in isolation in different service and technology teams, there is little opportunity for separating out activities except at a very low level.
Y	**2. CLIENT FOCUS** The service is at a high level in the structure in the support group and so can be represented to the client. However, development is separate and the service lead would be needed to coordinate development and support issues.
A	**3. RESOURCE FOCUS** Resource is mainly technology constrained. A given resource cannot work on different services as they are in different teams. Support resource also cannot work on development, however, support resource can work to different ITIL processes. Hence resource focus is narrow and may not have enough interest for retention.
Y	**4. KNOWLEDGE FOCUS** Service knowledge can be effectively retained by the service teams, although knowledge from development would need to be passed over. Technology knowledge is generated lower down and in isolation within a service. Tacit knowledge could be hard to retain.
R	**5. DEVELOPMENT FOCUS** Because the whole organisation is split at the highest level into development and support, communication and handover between these two groups is challenging.

Reframing ITIL

Option J- in Table 6.6

In our next considered organisational option the IT unit is split at the highest level between technologies. This effectively creates technology silos.

Each technology department is then split by major service, e.g. servers, networks, communications, and these are each split into development and support. All the service support teams each carry out the (relevant) IT processes such as incident management, problem management and request fulfilment.

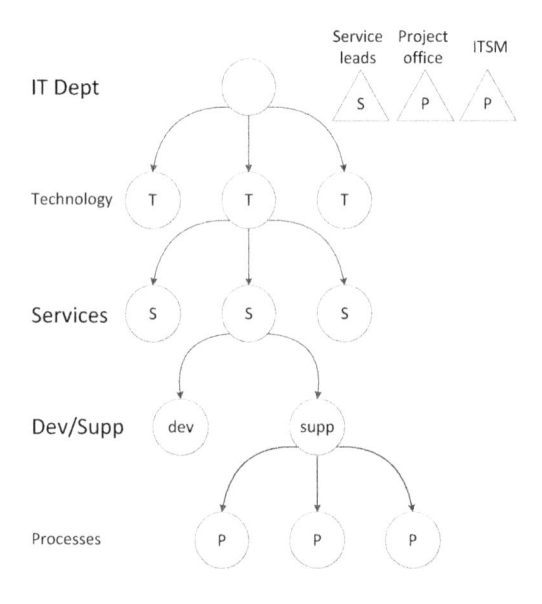

Figure 6.7 Blob diagram of organisation option J

As ITIL processes sit at the bottom of the organisation, there would be an ITSM unit to ensure coordination of the IT service processes between all the service-based support teams. There would certainly need to be coordination of services at the highest level to ensure consistency and provide an interface with the business/client. A project office would be needed at a high level to provide support and ensure consistency between the projects operating in the various technology and service-based development teams.

Chapter 6 – Designing the Service Organisation

So what are the issues with respect to the five criteria we have identified?

Table 6.4 RAYG assessment of organisation option J

RAYG	ISSUES
R	**1. END-USER FOCUS** All the support and development is grouped by technologies creating technology silos. This means that unless work is initially allocated correctly – and end users rarely know which technology they are using – it is hard to move to the right technology. With processes so low in the organisation, separation of low/high volume and complex activities would be very fragmented, and probably inconsistent.
A	**2. CLIENT FOCUS** Services sitting below technologies make it hard to coordinate all the work related to a single service in one place. This would reduce consistency and coherence. All coordination would need to be by the service leads.
G	**3. RESOURCE FOCUS** Although resource cannot easily move from technology to technology – which is unusual anyway – moves between processes are relatively easy providing flexibility and efficiency. Even moves between development and support are relatively easy here.
G	**4. KNOWLEDGE FOCUS** Technology knowledge can be effectively retained by the technology teams and includes development and support knowledge. Service knowledge is also at a high level. Process knowledge could be hard to retain.
G	**5. DEVELOPMENT FOCUS** Because service teams under technologies are split between development and support, it is relatively easy for these two activities to communicate or even share staff.

Reframing ITIL

Option L– in Table 6.6

In our last considered organisational option the IT unit is again split at the highest level between technologies. This again effectively creates technology silos.

Each technology department is then split into development and support groups and the support groups are split by ITIL processes. Only at the lowest level are services considered – as the numbers are so low, this would likely be at a person or even activity level.

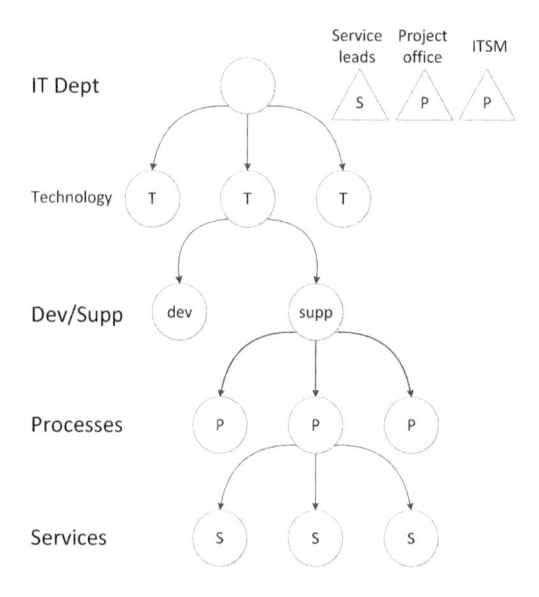

Figure 6.8 Blob diagram of organisation option L

There would certainly need to be coordination of services at the highest level to ensure some level of consistency and provide an interface with the business/client. As ITIL processes sit near the middle of the organisation, there would be an ITSM unit to ensure coordination of the IT service processes between all the technology-based support teams. A project office would probably sit at a high level to provide support and ensure consistency between the projects operating in the various technology-based development teams.

Chapter 6 – Designing the Service Organisation

So what are the issues with respect to the five criteria we have identified?

Table 6.5 RAYG assessment of organisation option L

RAYG	ISSUES
R	**1. END-USER FOCUS** All the support and development is grouped by technologies creating technology silos. This means that unless work is initially allocated correctly – and end users rarely know which technology they are using – it is hard to move to the right technology. Processes are placed next but the bottom position for services makes the organisation unresponsive. With processes so low in the organisation, separation of low/high volume and complex activities would be very fragmented, and probably inconsistent.
R	**2. CLIENT FOCUS** The bottom position for services makes it impossible to coordinate all the work related to a single service in one place. This would reduce consistency and coherence. All coordination would need to be by the Service leads.
G	**3. RESOURCE FOCUS** Although resource cannot easily move from technology to technology – which is unusual anyway – moves between services and processes are relatively easy providing flexibility and efficiency. Moves between development and support are less easy.
A	**4. KNOWLEDGE FOCUS** Although technology knowledge can be readily held, customer-focused, process and service knowledge would not be effectively retained.
Y	**5. DEVELOPMENT FOCUS** Because technology teams are split between development and support, it is not too hard for these two activities to communicate or even share staff, even though they may be divided by service.

Reframing ITIL

Table 6.6 RAYG assessments of all organisational options – highlighted options discussed in detail in sections above (A, D, H, J and L)

Org options below ICT dept.	1. END-USER responsiveness to..	2. CLIENT Strategic view and service coherence	3. RESOURCE - retention, flexiblity and efficency of use	4. KNOWLEDGE - retention and generation	5. DEVELOPMENT hand over	score	No. of reds
A Services / Technology / Dev/Supp / Processes	R	Y	Y	G	G	10	1
B Services / Dev/Supp / Technology / Processes	R	Y	A	Y	Y	13	1
C Services / Dev/Supp / Processes / Technology	A	G	R	A	A	14	1
D Dev/Supp / Processes / Services / Technology	G	A	R	R	R	16	3
E Dev/Supp / Processes / Technology / Services	G	R	Y	R	R	15	3
F Dev/Supp / Services / Processes / Technology	Y	Y	R	A	R	15	2
G Dev/Supp / Technology / Processes / Services	A	R	Y	A	R	16	2
H Dev/Supp / Services / Technology / Processes	R	Y	A	Y	R	15	2
I Dev/Supp / Technology / Services / Processes	R	R	Y	Y	R	16	3
J Technology / Services / Dev/Supp / Processes	R	A	G	G	G	10	1
K Technology / Dev/Supp / Services / Processes	R	A	G	Y	A	13	1
L Technology / Dev/Supp / Processes / Services	R	R	G	A	Y	14	2

Note that a lower score is better.

The whole matrix

Considering the whole matrix, all the thirteen organisational options that we are considering are listed on the left-hand side of Table 6.6 and lettered A to L. The five that we have discussed in more detail are highlighted in grey in the first column. The greyscale coding shows the extended RAYG system that we have used to assess the suitability of each organisational option from the perspective of the five organisational criteria.

To generate the score, the four RAYG options were scored 4 (red), 3 (amber), 2 (yellow) and 1 (green) and added together. Hence five reds would generate a score of 20 – the maximum – and five greens would generate a score of 5 – the minimum. The scores all group between 10 and 16 which is fairly central. All the options have at least one red criterion. Clearly then, using these criteria, there are no ideal organisational structures. Reality would tend to support this conclusion or most real IT support organisations would likely fit the best model.

Please note that those that were considered in detail (above) included the lowest scoring (best) – A and J – and three of the higher scoring (worst) – D, H and L.

Before looking further at the best options, we should ask whether there are some general conclusions that can be drawn. The answer would appear to be yes and they are given here:

What is needed for good end-user responsiveness? (1.)

To identify what is needed for good end-user responsiveness, we need to be clear what is of importance to the typical end user.

For most end-users using the services, it is important to have an easy and clear access to the operational processes that are directly used by end users – namely request fulfilment, incident management or general queries. It is also useful to have a quick and routine process for simple queries and a more appropriate process for more involved queries. This works best if routine (=low-complexity), high-volume activities are dealt with separately from complex, low-volume activities.

To achieve this in these simple, model organisations, the processes (i.e. request fulfilment, incident management) need to be high up in the organisation for first contact. Once this contact has been made, each needs good access to service and technology staff to resolve the queries.

What is needed for good client focus? (2.)
To identify what is needed for good client focus we need to clarify what is important to the typical client.

For clients, it is important to have an interface with a single point of contact who/which can coordinate a coherent view of each service, combining both strategic and operational aspects. Ideally, from the client's point of view, this 'service lead' should have complete (line) responsibility for the service in all its aspects – through development and support.

To achieve this, the service level needs to be at the top of the organisation. If this cannot be achieved, then it needs to be as high as possible. This enables the service lead to report, change and manage a service as the client requires.

What is needed for good resource focus? (3.)
To identify what is needed for good resource focus we need to clarify what delivers an effective focus on the resource (people) so that the organisation can retain critical staff and expertise. Part of this, and also an issue for efficiency, is whether resources can move easily to other work to ensure they are not under (or over) utilised.

Operational resource tends to be technology focused. Interest in this work often comes from working on a variety of different problems and this may come from the ability to work at different levels of complexity – easy incidents, hard incidents, problems, even development work. Interest may also come from the ability to move between working on different services, which present different types of work but all within the technology area of interest.

To achieve this, technology needs to be at a high level in the organisation. This allows all the flexibility below it for movement between processes and/or services groups.

What is needed for effective knowledge management? (4.)
We need to identify how effectively the organisational structure encourages knowledge generation and retention. In this we are talking mainly about implicit knowledge and expertise held by people, rather than information held in so-called 'knowledge bases', but actually databases or information systems.

The two most important types of knowledge for delivering a high quality of support or development are technology knowledge or knowledge of the client's service (business knowledge).

Within these two types, knowledge is developed and deepened when resources get an opportunity to work in a variety of areas. This occurs best when technology is at a high organisational level or services are at a high organisational level – delivering the two respective knowledge areas.

What is needed for effective development? (5.)
We need to identify how effectively the organisational structure encourages effective transfer of a development project through all its stages and across organisational boundaries into live support.

Delivering services that are easy to support, requires a close relationship between developers and support staff – perhaps even some development may be done by support staff. Handover from one stage to the next is also easiest if organisational units are close – ideally in the same group.

For this to happen, the development/support split needs to be as low down in the organisation as possible.

Conclusion
It is fairly apparent that, perhaps not surprisingly, what is needed for each of these criteria is quite different! This means that any successful organisation is going to be a compromise and perhaps the different criteria need to be prioritised for a given set of requirements to best meet them. However, there are more things that can be done.

Adding reality to the organisational types

The investigation so far has established that none of the basic organisational structures can deliver perfect, or indeed, particularly effective, large client service organisations in themselves. To move further in this direction, special accommodations need to be made and functions and coordination need to be added or considered.

Reframing ITIL

Table 6.7   RAYG assessments of all organisational options – highlighted options discussed in more detail. Incorporates a service desk.

	Org options below ICT dept.	correct first referral to technology group	2. CLIENT Strategic view and service coherence	3. RESOURCE - retention, flexiliblty and efficency of use	4. KNOWLEDGE - retention and generation	5. DEVELOPMENT hand over	score	No. of reds
A	Services / Technology / Dev/Supp / Processes	G	Y	Y	G	G	7	0
B	Services / Dev/Supp / Technology / Processes	G	Y	A	Y	Y	10	0
C	Services / Dev/Supp / Processes / Technology	G	G	R	A	A	12	1
D	Dev/Supp / Processes / Services / Technology	G	A	R	R	R	16	3
E	Dev/Supp / Processes / Technology / Services	A	R	Y	R	R	17	3
F	Dev/Supp / Services / Processes / Technology	G	Y	R	A	R	14	2
G	Dev/Supp / Technology / Processes / Services	A	R	Y	A	R	16	2
H	Dev/Supp / Services / Technology / Processes	G	Y	A	Y	R	12	1
I	Dev/Supp / Technology / Services / Processes	A	R	Y	Y	R	15	2
J	Technology / Services / Dev/Supp / Processes	A	A	G	G	G	9	0
K	Technology / Dev/Supp / Services / Processes	A	A	G	Y	A	12	0
L	Technology / Dev/Supp / Processes / Services	A	R	G	A	Y	13	1

114

A Service desk

A major additional feature comes by including one of the ITIL functions – a contact or service desk – discussed in Chapter 2. When this is included it replaces the original 'End-user focus' column in Table 6.7.

Regardless of where the service desk sits nominally in the organisation – and it is a support function so would usually sit in support – it considerably changes 'End-user focus'. It immediately gives the end user a better experience, by providing a single point of contact. Some issues can now be resolved centrally – such as first-time fixes for simple incidents, advice given on common questions and standard requests can be fulfilled.

The contact desk is normally supported by workflow software that the contact desk staff uses to ensure that issues get passed to the correct groups and that responses are tracked and closed. This was discussed in Chapter 2 in some detail.

For slightly more complex issues, the service the end user gets will depend on the ease of contacting the correct technology group to resolve them. Although there are many factors that can impact this – see Chapter 2 – the organisational component is whether the service sits above technology or not.

If the service sits above technology, the contact desk can pass a query to the service layer who can then move it between the technologies until the correct group is found. The contact desk knows the correct service because the query will have referenced the service – however, the user rarely knows the technology.

If technology sits above service, then the contact desk needs to work out the technology required and frequently gets this wrong. This results in increased incorrect first referrals of the query to the technology group. In reality this can result in over half the queries being misdirected.

However, taking these points into account, having a contact desk still considerably simplifies the matrix as shown below and removes all the red criteria from the end-user column – now retitled "correct first referral to technology group" to reflect the points just made.

Reframing ITIL

Coordination mechanisms

In the various organisations considered, there are also *coordination mechanisms* – often departments – that ensure that if the line management cannot adequately manage, an alternative is available. Some of these are shown in Figures 6.4 to 6.8.

The main such departments include an ITSM (IT Service Management) group, a project office, technology leads/architects and service leads or liaison managers. There are also service design packs and knowledge bases. What then is the role of each of these? They are given in detail in the ITIL books, but a brief summary here may help:

IT Service Management (ITSM)

The ITSM department normally includes the 'owners' of each of the ITIL processes which, as we have seen in Chapters 2, 3, 4 and 5, are very varied. Although some of the processes are carried out within the ITSM team and, in large organisations, sub-teams are sometimes present doing processes such as security or knowledge management, much of the operational process activity is pure coordination – in the form of making sure that process documentation is available and monitoring the performance of the processes to ensure the service agreements are met.

Project office (PMO)

The project office owns all the project management processes used in the development group (and elsewhere if relevant). It would normally also provide resources to coordinate monitoring the ongoing projects and how they are performing against plans. The project management methodologies, documentation and templates are also owned here to ensure that all the projects work to the same standards. Resources may also be available for programme management of multiple, linked projects.

Technology leads / architects

Although technology leads and systems architects are not synonymous, it is very common to have a Chief Technology Officer with a group of systems (IT systems for once!) architects working for them. Frequently the architects have technology responsibilities making them technology leads. Their main activity is in the Service Design and Transition spaces where they prepare plans and documentation for new and significantly revised services. They ensure that all services meet the same standards and are compatible with each other and the encompassing system. Alongside the technical architects in larger IT departments or accounts, it is possible to find service support architects (by some name) who define and document the processes and resources that support the services once they have gone live.

Service design pack (SDP)
Perhaps realising that the common structures used in IT development and support organisations do not encourage end-to-end development and support, ITIL describes the 'service design pack' in some detail – see Chapter 3. This is frequently owned by architects or service leads. Its purpose is to hold all the documentation from design to implementation that is required to develop and support a service. If implemented effectively it can have a significant moderating effect on the tendency to 'throw projects over organisation walls'. Particularly in organisational options D through I, it is the SDP that holds the development cycle together. Unfortunately, SDPs are rarely implemented effectively, if at all, and so this simple fix is neglected.

Service leads / service liaison managers
Where there are large services, it is common for service leads to act in the liaison space with the business customer, collecting requirements and reporting progress and performance. They also work to ensure that the service being delivered – from planning through development to support – is as required. In some organisations they have a line management role to development and support staff, but just as commonly they must try and coordinate resource owned by other departments.

Knowledge bases
Knowledge base is a term used in ITIL, however as an electronic system can only ever hold explicit knowledge, they would better be termed information systems or even databases. They act to store information about the services and frequently observed incidents or queries, including known errors. This is entered by contact desk staff or technical support staff for the use of other contact desk staff or even the end users directly.

The burden of coordination
Coordination does not come without adding a burden to the organisation and it is frequently less than perfect. The greater the number of organisational boundaries across which coordination takes place, the higher the burden on the coordinator and the lower the chance of coordination being effective. Hence coordination of any type can be more of a challenge in some organisational structures than others. This is again a matrix and again we will attempt to

Reframing ITIL

analyse it – but to keep it manageable, we will look only at the five organisational options we have so far focused on. Scoring is slightly different and accommodates the slightly lower significance of these items as compared to the line management ones shown in Table 6.6 and 6.7. Here red is scored 3, amber 2 (there is no yellow) and green 1. The RAG refers to effectiveness.

Table 6.8 RAG assessments of *coordination* options for selected options discussed in detail above.

The Burden of Coordination

Org options below ICT dept.	ITSM	Project office	Service Leads	Tech Leads	score	No. of reds
A Services Technology Dev/Supp Processes	R	R		A	8	2
D Dev/Supp Processes Services Technology	G		A	R	6	1
H Dev/Supp Services Technology Processes	R	G	G	A	7	1
J Technology Services Dev/Supp Processes	R	R	A		8	2
L Technology Dev/Supp Processes Services	A	A	R		7	1

Note that there are gaps – these occur where the 'coordination activity' actually becomes the line management – as in service leads being the line managers in organisation option A.

Where this is not the case, and as one might expect, there is a greater burden of *coordination* when the activities/departments being coordinated are split out lower down the organisation. As an example, *coordination* carried out by service leads is relatively easy in organisation option H where services are grouped organisationally just below the top development/support split. At the other extreme, in organisation type L, the organisation is only split by services at the very bottom level, meaning that the service leads have to coordinate numerous small departments for each service.

However great the burden, coordination can never be as effective as line management in ensuring the smooth running of an organisation because it does not have access to the purse strings – the resource negotiation loop – but has to act indirectly through the line management wherever resource issues are concerned.

What is the best organisational option?

Now we come to the big question – what is the best option from an organisational perspective? If there were an easy or obvious answer IT staff would (probably) all be working in the same type of organisation and this is certainly not the case. However, we do now have the information that should let us choose options knowing the advantages and disadvantages each would confer in a given situation.

The table (Table 6.9 below) that summarises the findings is, however, rather ambiguous. Even allowing that it might be thought that we have combined 'apples and pears' by summing the scores from line management and coordination, the outcome is still unclear. The potential theoretical best scores might be considered as 8 and the worst as 28 (this is arguable as not all combinations are possible). The actual scores here range from 15 to 22 which lie either side of the half-way point. Please note that we have confirmed that none of the options that have *not* been looked at here (i.e. from the whole of A through L) are better.

There is no clear winner, but **option A** is the favourite (lowest scores), with service leads taking the highest management position below the top level. development and support would be closely integrated here. In this organisation, the ITSM group and the project office could be challenged to ensure that standards in support and development, respectively, are maintained.

Option D has the poorest score of these five and nearly the poorest score overall (there is one higher score, of 23 – option E). It also has four red scores, three in line management. There is a high level split between development and support – which is not uncommon in reality – but the next level split out into processes is less common. Although the end user is well served, the client would be less happy and resource and knowledge retention and development are exceptionally poor. Handover of new and improved services from development to support would be a challenge, as would the maintenance of technology standards and approaches.

Reframing ITIL

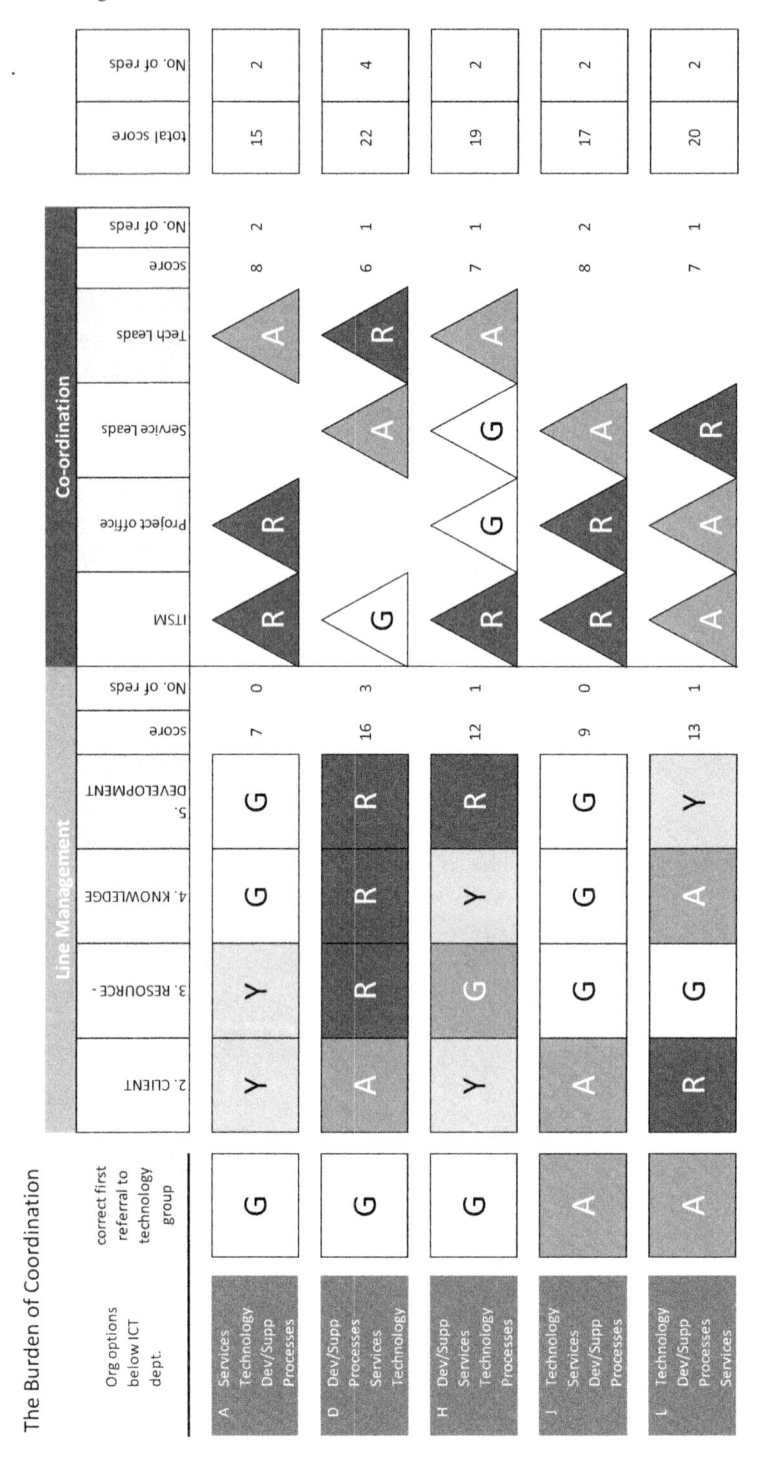

Table 6.9 RAYG assessments of selected organisational options including coordination options and incorporating a service desk

120

Option H is of particular interest because it arguably most closely resembles many real IT departments – especially outsourced ones. Development is hived off into a separate department at the highest level and would hence struggle to integrate with live services. Once development is out of the way, the organisation resembles A: with services next and technology and processes below. If service leads run the services groups, then they would only be managing the support functions directly and may struggle to get development work prioritised. ITSM would almost certainly sit at the same level and could be challenged to ensure that standards in support processes are maintained.

Option J is rather different in that with the high-level technology split, it may not be able to deliver as well to the end users or clients (who are more interested in services). However, it is much better for the 'internal' aspects of the organisation: namely resource efficiency and retention, knowledge generation and retention and joined-up development. ITSM and project offices would both struggle to ensure that standards in support and development, respectively, are maintained.

Option L again has a high level technology split, but each technology group is then split into development and support above the service level, so joined-up development would be a challenge. Operational processes come next in the support group and services last. This would make the service lead job particularly hard and the client would not be well served; end users could also be unhappy.

It seems probable that at this stage we have gone as far as we realistically can with these 'theoretical' organisations, although you may have spotted some that resemble your own and garnered some insights from this. It is time to look at some examples of real organisations that some of our associates have experienced and see how they manage to work. We will leave a range of additional problems principally associated with outsourcing to the next chapter.

Some real organisations

ITIL introduces the supporting organisation as service operation functions. At a high level these are split into the service desk, technical management and applications management. In most real organisations, the technical and applications management functions are grouped into a relatively small number of 'towers'. It is a bit debatable whether towers represent services or technologies – perhaps both. For the purposes of this discussion towers will be considered to represent technologies at a high level.

There is usually an applications tower and then the technical management functions are grouped into infrastructure towers – often between three and six in total.

Although some applications, such as those for finance and HR, may be considered to be shared services – i.e. they are used throughout the organisation – more applications are used specifically by individual business groups or even customers of the parent organisation. By contrast, nearly all of the technical/infrastructure functions are shared services used by the whole organisation.

Large outsourced IT account 1

Our first real organisation is a large, outsourced, private sector, IT account. It has a structure that is a cross between options E and L. There is a high level technology split into three towers. The one focused on here is the applications tower which, uniquely of the three towers, was split at this level into a development tower and a support tower. This reflects the relative effort going into development for applications as compared to infrastructure.

At the highest level there is a contact desk, for end users to access support, which delivers '1st line' incident support, standard request fulfilment and information provision across all the technologies.

There is also an ITSM group at this highest level which coordinates the ITIL process standards between the technologies, although they are then picked up by each technology support group and made real.

The T3 support groups have operational process divisions: incident management (2nd line), incident management (3rd line) and problem management, and test/release management. Under these process divisions the 3rd line and problem teams are focused on a given technology, broken down by service or – in the case of the technologically less demanding 2nd line – by geography.

The main problems with this approach were:

1. The technology towers became very isolated from each other and any collaborative working on issues was difficult.

Chapter 6 – Designing the Service Organisation

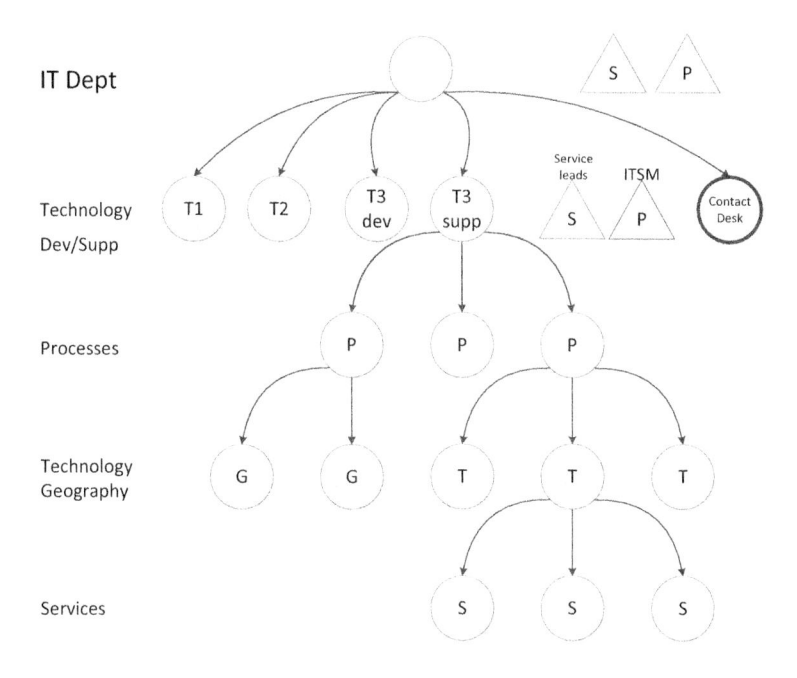

Figure 6.9 Blob diagram of a large IT account

2. The development of new services within each tower was disconnected from the support activities and frequently the services as delivered were almost unusable. This frustrated the support staff and caused client dissatisfaction.

3. The staff (resource) didn't like the process split as it reduced the variety in their day-to-day work. Those doing the least varied work (2nd line) found it particularly unsatisfactory.

4. The contact desk recruited poorly paid staff and there was high turnover. Knowledge transfer from the technology towers was inadequate and the end-user service was poor.

5. There was a lack of clarity about who had responsibility for processes between the ITSM groups in the towers and at the higher level.

Reframing ITIL

The hybrid nature of the organisation – with technology split at two levels and different processes divided up in different ways – is not uncommon and can take advantage of slightly different requirements in different areas. The technology in focus (T3) carried out a much higher proportion of development work than the other towers – not atypical of applications – which justified the high-level split into two towers, T3 development and T3 support.

The T3 support tower (applications) organisation was later changed to the following which resembles option H:

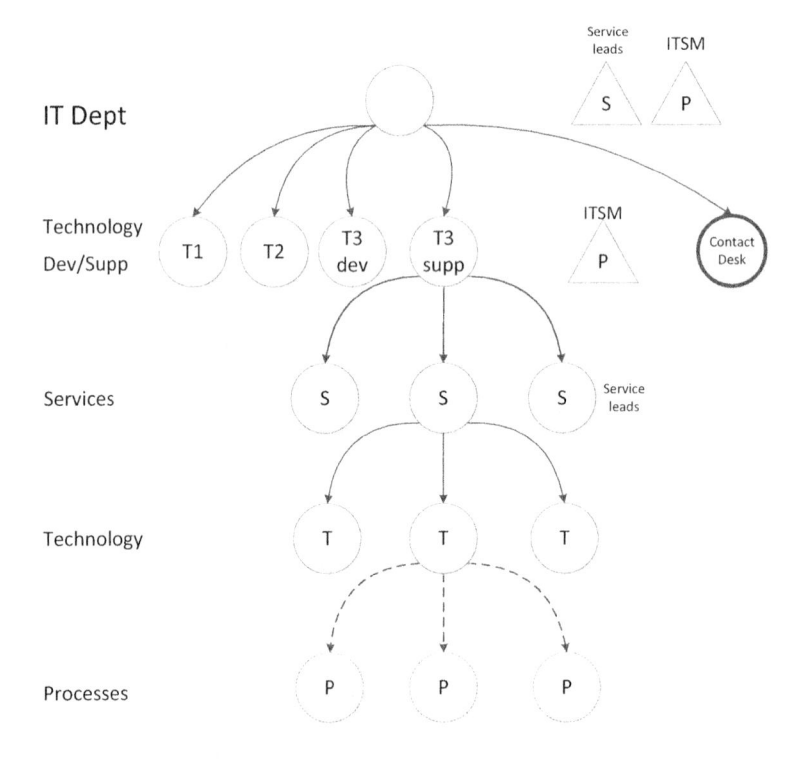

Figure 6.10 Blob diagram of a large IT account (modified)

The operational process split was removed as it had been unpopular. Instead, service leads were given higher-level budgeting authority and although this wasn't shown on the organisation chart, the de facto organisation became as shown.

The operational processes were all now carried out in the technology teams hence the dotted structure.

Chapter 6 – Designing the Service Organisation

Within the T3 support group this proved more successful although the problems with application development (T3 dev) delivering unsupportable services continued – the service leads in the T3 support tower having little influence there.

It is worth noting that the high-level structure of 'towers' is widely found in large IT support organisations as this makes it easier to outsource the various towers to a number of different outsource suppliers.

Large outsourced IT account 2

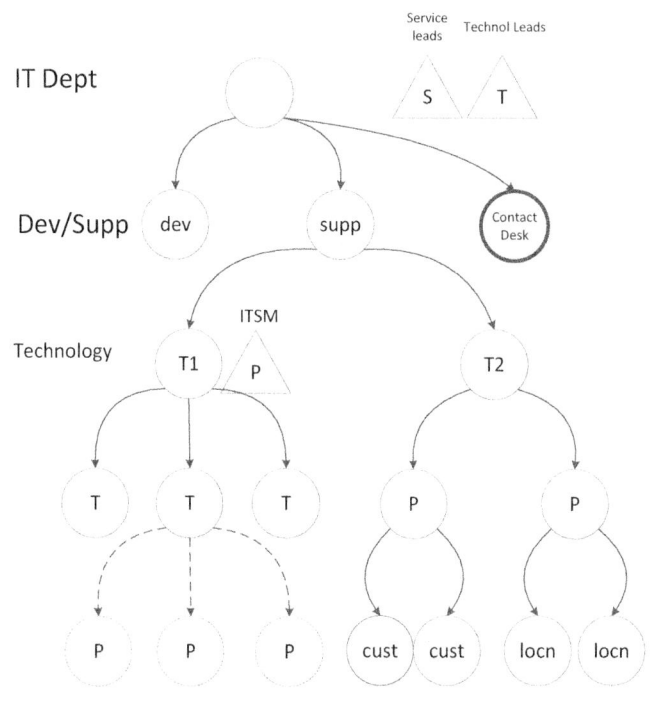

Figure 6.11 Blob diagram of a large account

Our second real organisation is a large, outsourced, public-sector IT account. It has a structure that is a cross between options G and I. There is again a high-level split into development and support and the support division is then split into two towers by technology, one for technical management and one for application management – quite a common division of labour.

The technical management tower (T1) was split by technology teams which each carried out all the required operational processes.

By contrast, the application tower (T2) was split by operational process – the simpler incident processes being split by grade of customer and the more complex problem and request processes being split by location.

There was a contact desk at a high level feeding incidents and requests to the appropriate teams. ITSM sat in the technical management tower.

The main problems with this approach were:

1. The development of new services was disconnected from the support activities in each tower and frequently the services as delivered were almost unusable. This frustrated the support staff and caused client dissatisfaction.

2. The two technology towers became isolated from each other and collaborative working on issues was difficult.

3. The service leads had no line responsibility and so struggled to get a rapid, resourced response to client concerns from the delivery and support groups.

4. The contact desk recruited poorly paid staff and there was high turnover – knowledge transfer from the technology towers was inadequate and the end-user service was poor.

5. The position of the ITSM group within the technical management tower caused some disquiet in the other technology tower and resistance to following process.

Note that the split of different towers in different ways is quite common. This is especially the case if these towers are being managed by different outsourcing companies who follow their own internal preferences and styles.

Conclusions

It is fairly clear that it has not proved possible to identify an 'ideal' organisational structure for providing IT support in large organisations using the viable system methodology. However, the factors that affect choosing organisational structures have been identified and the problems with particular structures have also become clearer. This means that intelligent choices can be made and organisations can be designed to meet the highest priority needs –

Chapter 6 – Designing the Service Organisation

whatever they are deemed to be. Further, where imperfect choices are made – and they always will be – compensating mechanisms can be built in and the inevitable problems can be monitored for and mitigated.

Many IT organisations use organisational diagrams that show a matrix in an attempt to reconcile the conflicting demands discussed above. However, whenever these are investigated in detail it is found that only one dimension provides the resource and the other(s) operate through *coordination* mechanisms. Because this is not understood, confusion can occur.

A side effect of the lack of a single, ideal organisation and of not understanding that such is impossible is the continuous search for such an organisation. This is the cause of the continual reorganisations that are the bane of many IT organisations (and others, of course). Unfortunately these reorganisations can result more in unnecessary cost and confusion rather than improvement. Contrary to this is the 'reorganisation effect' which has been found to result in increased productivity regardless of the before and after structures. Such reorganisations may result in a more appropriate structure but this is usually by chance rather than design.

The focus of this chapter has been large IT organisations, principally outsourced ones. The issues of smaller organisations are different only in scale and sometimes the sequence of organisational options is more implied than implemented in units and departments, being carried out by small teams or even individuals.

The structures of outsourced organisations supporting large numbers of small clients have different issues, although still following the same principles, and these are not discussed here.

How do the management processes fit?
The management processes described in Chapter 5 as 'Managing the Service Organisation' apply at the IT Department level (and above if so indicated in Chapter 5) in all the theoretical and real examples above.

The management processes described in Chapter 4 as 'Managing the Service' apply to ALL the levels below this, regardless of whether Service is the next level down in a given case.

Approximate meaning of RAYG scale

- Red = efficiency and effectiveness are drastically affected by the organisational structure, causing potentially customer contract delivery deficiencies and financially damages, and/or reducing efficiency by up to 80%

- Amber = efficiency and effectiveness are adversely impacted by the organisational structure, causing potential major customer service issues and/or reducing efficiency by up to 50%

- Yellow = efficiency and effectiveness are affected by the organisational structure, causing potential minor customer service issues and/or reducing efficiency by up to 20%

- Green = everything will work really effectively and efficiently.

Chapter 7

Outsourcing the Service

– organisational issues of the second kind

As we near the end of this reframing, it is appropriate to look at outsourcing. Although outsourcing isn't ITIL, ITIL clearly anticipates that a lot of IT services will be delivered by outsourced IT departments. Regardless of this, outsourcing provides lots of interesting organisational and process issues which merit investigation and framing.

There are two extremes of outsourcing – which graduate into each other. At the simpler end is the case where discrete, standard services are outsourced to a single supplier. At the other extreme, a large organisation might outsource its whole IT department – requiring a more bespoke solution!

Standard service outsourcing

Starting with the outsourcing of standard services (an example might be a telephony service). Such services can generally be 'bought off the shelf'. Domestically we do this all the time, when we buy an internet service, or a computer, or a piece of software – we're buying a standard service offering. In general, and complaints about ISPs notwithstanding, this is usually a more successful tactic than trying to build any of these services ourselves!

What largely characterises the success of these services is that they are standard – we all buy the same, or at least a similar, service with little or no customisation. As the purchaser, we do not interfere with the service provided, or see the need to closely monitor the service provider. The provider can therefore 'do it their way' and focus on economies of scale.

Smaller organisations may choose to 'buy' their whole IT provision in this way and make do with the vanilla services that a large service provider can deliver. This can be successful if the client organisation is flexible enough to modify its processes to match the IT services it receives.

Whole IT department outsourcing

If a large organisation outsources its whole IT department it expects to have its whole, customised and bespoke, set of applications, infrastructure and business knowledge managed for it – but of course at lower cost and with higher performance and professionalism than if it were doing it itself! The outsource provider is expected – and expects – to do this successfully by applying its own, standardised infrastructure and application development resources. Herein lies the first problem:

If the highly bespoke and customised requirements are clearly defined in the request to tender, then any realistic bids are likely to be too high to get the work.

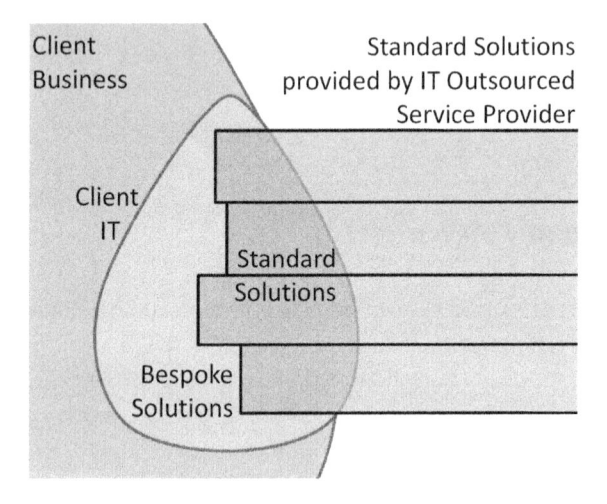

Figure 7.1: The standard solutions provided by the IT outsourced service provider cannot fill the needs of the client IT. There is still a gap that requires some bespoke solutions, even if not described as such

Fortunately (?) however, those involved in pricing the bids don't usually have the understanding of the costs incurred when there is a move away from the standard solution, so they underbid and their bid is accepted. Thus is the work allocated and the contract finalised!

Chapter 7 – Outsourcing the Service

So, at the start there is frequently a conflict of expectations. Once the outsource provider's technical and business people get involved, they can find themselves in a cleft stick. They're trapped between the requirements of the client – sometimes described in the contract – and the standard approaches they are expected to use by their parent organisation to deliver the economies of scale on which the price was based: It can't be done.

The diagram in Figure 7.1 shows that the outsourced service provider has to provide enough resource or capability to fit the client's bespoke requirements, as well as the standard requirements that they were expecting. Many providers simply don't have the available resource and don't do this adequately.

In practice, even as little as 10% of non-standard services can more than double the cost of delivering a contract. This fact seems to be unknown to many sales professionals and contract negotiators, so even if they do recognise the non-standard nature of some services, they don't appreciate the scale and cost of the impact. They exacerbate this blind spot, frequently failing to carry out the necessary due diligence with the servicing arms of their own organisation, or worse, incorporating capabilities without the associated costs in pursuit of an acceptable bid price.

The problems that whole IT department outsourcing without an adequate understanding of bespoke requirements can produce may be much reduced if:

- The outsourced service provider has a clear and structured portfolio – including both standard services AND the cost of supporting bespoke and customised services. These can then more easily be matched to requirements – and realistically costed.

- The outsourced service provider performs due diligence on contract details – and so does the client – prior to final contract signature, not afterwards.

- The outsourced service provider identifies and challenges all bespoke requirements in the request for tender – indicating the true costs.

- The client challenges the outsourced service provider to ensure a common, full understanding of the services required and conducts their own due diligence of the response.

Finally, and critically,

- The outsourced service provider invests in groups of staff able to support bespoke and customised infrastructure, applications and other services – probably, initially including transitioned staff for each account.

Behind these fixes is a bigger one – the outsourced service provider needs to become a learning organisation so that the lessons of unsuccessful contracting are correctly learned and measures, such as those above, are put in place to make future contracts more successful. However, for some outsourcing organisations, changing from a 'we reinvent wheels' to a learning organisation mode is just too big an ask. Culture at this level is VERY hard to change.

Building a business from scratch

"The new service provider is delivering the outsourced service; everyone is keeping their heads down and doing their job delivering to the client. Under the surface, however, all is not well: Staff are not sure who to ask about things, the tooling is not behaving, their role may be growing but there is no way to get additional resource; they are not rewarded for working long hours and may not even be sure who they report to. Demotivation is growing and key staff are starting to leave for greener pastures. The posts they vacate are not filled. Managers don't have the information they need to be sure things are running smoothly, don't know how many staff they have or who they are and ever more frequently a nasty surprise arrives which cannot always be kept from the client. The more forceful and aggressive managers (the 'heroes') begin to take control while everyone else feels as though they are wading through a swamp. This is all because the support organisation has not been assembled properly."

So, this second issue for focus is perhaps less obvious and more variable between outsourced service providers: it is to do with the structure and organisation of the outsourced IT department – or account – from the perspective of the outsourced service provider. This applies whether the outsourcing is of standard or bespoke services, so long as the support organisation is large. There has been substantial discussion of this in Chapter 6.

An account may be a substantial organisation in its own right – especially if supporting a government department or large private business. However, unlike large commercial organisations, it will usually have been created, or recreated, pretty much from scratch.

In the outside business world, organisations grow – partly planned, partly ad hoc – some slowly, some fast. Interfaces and management usually emerge over time. Poor organisational structure and process can be the cause of business failure. Therefore those businesses that succeed have, by definition, organisations that at least suffice to support the business through good times and bad – they are viable. There is no such opportunity for weeding out poor account organisations in the outsourcing world.

Successful organisations have two key, mutually integrated, characteristics: they are stable and they are adaptable, and they can change themselves. The absence of even a single component in the spectrum of characteristics, due to poor design, can cause a rapid proliferation of errors if the wrong button is pushed and catastrophic failure then ensues. This frequently pushes the organisation into a new operating mode which is even less adaptable.

Structural viability

So long as there are no significant challenges or changes, it is surprisingly common for outsourced IT to carry on delivering an adequate service even when the organisation around it is functionally almost non-existent. This, of course, can only occur while the original – outsourced – IT staff are still around. Everyone keeps their eyes down and focuses on their job. Hence the stability requirement is being maintained.

If anything bigger than their job comes up, that's when the problems arise. This is normally when the adaptability requirement becomes evident. If the structures and processes aren't there to handle unexpected variety in demand from clients, then the problems start.

A major purpose of any organisation is to ensure that the work its staff do – the delivery – is aligned. This is maintained by various types of communication which are partly driven by a set of organisational systems that are needed at *each level* of management. At higher levels of management there may be whole departments for each of these – at lower levels, a single individual may need to carry out all of them in parallel!

In the next parts, some of these structures and processes are discussed. They were originally introduced in a different context back in Chapter 4 and similar nomenclature will be used. Please see this as a refresher.

Reframing ITIL

Management

Management need a system for directing and requesting work, for providing the resource for that work and for measuring how well it is being done. This is well understood and is what most people think of as *management*.

However, for this to work there need to be a number of things happening:

- Managers need to receive management information, i.e. the information they need to understand how well the work is being done. This can involve considerable forethought to ensure that the right information is summarised for the manager and at the right level of detail. Agreeing a common format, structure and flow for this monitoring information can save a lot of time. If an essential feature of the work is not summarised in the management information, then it is invisible to the manager and can go badly awry, before becoming evident, and may cause major problems.

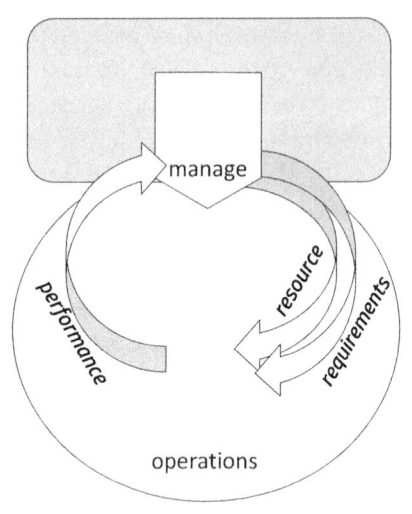

Figure 7.2 The *management* system at a single level in an organisation

- Management need to make sure that they don't just review the management information, but they make decisions based on it to remedy issues and make improvements. This sounds obvious, but is too frequently not done – especially with less experienced managers.

- In many cases, there needs to be regular meetings of a manager with their group of staff managers to present and review the monitoring information, allowing comparison of actual results with capability expectations. This allows unclear information to be discussed and clarified before decisions are taken. It also makes sure that the staff managers are aligned in their thinking and planning. Time needs to be allowed in the diary for these meetings to happen.

- These regular meetings should be arranged to that they happen up and down the organisation in a sequence over a time period – such as a week, a month or a quarter. This provides a regular cycle for managing the organisation and needs to be adaptable to the transactions carried out by different departments, as well as the criticality of particular contractual elements to the client.

- For this to be most effective, the system should ensure that decisions are taken by the management at the appropriate level of the organisation. Without this, senior management find their whole time taken up with operational minutiae. This is a significant cause of organisational failure: Senior managers cannot have enough insight and knowledge to make the right decisions on detailed operational issues and will get many wrong; senior managers doing this will not spend enough time on the more strategic matters they should be addressing.

Monitoring, or management by walking about

There is a related but subtly different system: It is most commonly known as *management by walking about*. Although this is most commonly seen as a management style, it is actually a quite different system all together and supports the reporting part of management seen above.

All the parts of *management* assume that the information being provided by reporting is relevant, complete and truthful. In the real world, it is common – indeed perhaps even normal practice, for lower level-managers to gently mislead their bosses about the success of their particular unit. This is a form of gaming. It is about presenting the good news and hiding the bad. At worst the reporting systems are corrupted to make sure this happens; the information selected for management reporting excludes the difficult and problematic factors. This is so common that little is seen to be wrong with it, and this behaviour frequently arises in organisations where there is 'fear' of passing bad news upwards, or where the messengers are (metaphorically) shot.

As a result, managers receiving such filtered information do not have the basis to make the right decisions. They can, however, largely pre-empt this dangerous situation by using a *management by walking about* approach. They take the time to look round the organisation and talk to the operational staff – bypassing their immediate staff management – to find out what is really happening. This is a form of monitoring and can be amazingly effective. It not only ensures that they are better informed, it also motivates the operational staff, who now knows that their concerns are reaching those who can act on them. Even when the manager is satisfied that the management information they are receiving is accurate and representative, this still has value and often represents the only safe upwards 'feedback' mechanism.

Coordination

A second system that management need is one that provides standards and practices for the subsidiary groups to use to make sure that they all work in an aligned and joined-up way. This system is known as *co-ordination*. This reduces the tendency for teams or departments to 'go their own way' – each developing their own preferred ways of doing things. Although there may be a place for this, it is important that many things are done the same way.

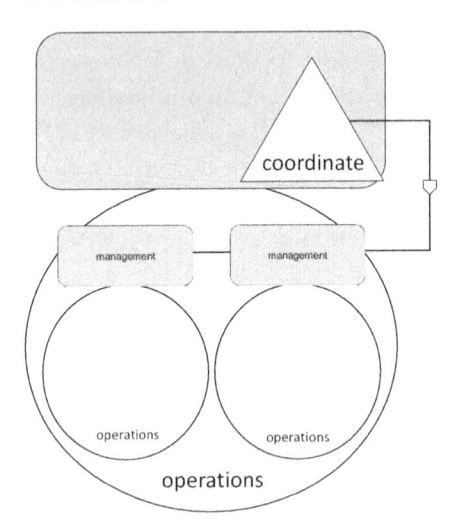

Figure 7.3 The *coordination* system at a single level in an organisation

Imagine, at an extreme, an international company where each department decided on a different core language to work in – the departments wouldn't be able to communicate with each other. In organisations that have been formed by amalgamation – and that can include outsourced staff working for a new set of managers – business language and its interpretation can be quite different. The adoption of IT Infrastructure Library (ITIL) guidelines by so many working in IT is often an attempt to reduce this issue, although it's critical that ITIL is used consistently, otherwise the terminology and approach can result in different barriers and 'cliques', sometimes between ITIL adopters and other staff.

Other standards can include financial reporting standards, process standards, salary policy – the list is endless and most modern companies just assume this happens. However, when an organisation is set up from scratch – like an account – it is not uncommon for some standards and practices to be missing and this, again, can cause things to go awry.

Innovation

The *management* system and the *coordination* system both have focus on the organisation as it is now, on making sure it is delivering what is required. However all organisations also need *innovation;* to plan for the future, look out for what is coming from outside, ensure that there is research and development going on, and that development is responding effectively to changing demand from the service provider's market place and clients.

In outsourced IT this function is fulfilled by three groups. The first is the architects who are looking for new technological initiatives – from both inside the main outsourcing organisation and also from suppliers.

The second is normally fulfilled by sales or business relationship managers, by whatever name – these look into requirements from or possibilities in the client business. In both cases the aim would be to generate new programmes of work to bring new services to the client.

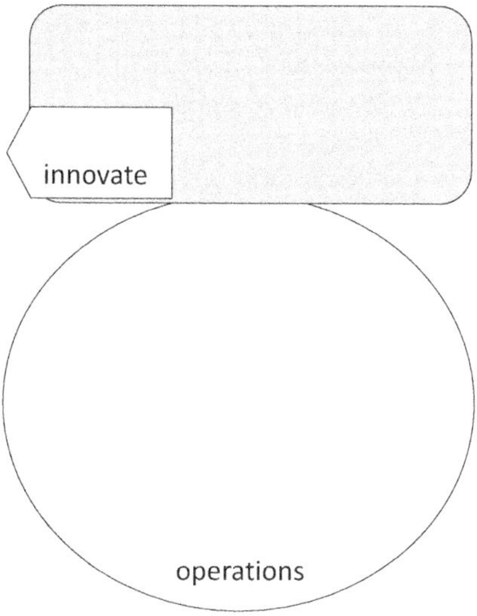

Figure 7.4 The *innovation* system at a single level in an organisation

A third group also has a focus on the future – this is the improvement group who are looking for opportunities to improve existing services through reorganisation, redefinition of processes, revised services, new tooling etc.. Again the aim is to get the client to approve new work programmes. In exceptional cases where reduced costs are expected, the outsourced service provider could provide the resourcing itself.

Introducing processes from scratch

Setting up an outsourced IT organisation also requires that all the processes also be set up. This is where ITIL comes in and indeed ITIL processes are the ones that are most frequently implemented. As shown in Chapters 1 through 5, ITIL does provide a template for many of the processes required.

Of the ITIL processes already introduced in this book, the typical operational ITIL implementation includes incident management, request fulfilment and service desks (a function in ITIL, not a process) which provide a customer face. Service level management is usually also implemented, although not always automated, as this is the basis of most contractual obligations through monitoring the performance of the customer-facing processes.

In the warranty space, availability management is usually implemented which, coupled with monitoring, also provides information for the availability and IT performance service levels. It is usual for security management and IT service continuity management also to be active.

Finally, some form of change management is essential to ensure that the live service remains uncompromised, although this is frequently only active in the operational (i.e. not the development project) area.

This selection of processes provides the bare minimum for providing support to IT services. Even when others are specified in a contract, they may not be effectively implemented. There are many important processes missing from this list and the following discussion will attempt to identify the key ones.

Partial implementation of ITIL

Problem management is one of the processes which is likely to be agreed contractually but not implemented effectively. Problem management is important for both client and outsource provider alike as it provides a gradual fixing of problems which results in improvements to the service, the reduction of incidents and hence the reduction of costs.

If an outsource provider is paid on a 'per incident' basis, then this immediately reduces motivation to implement effective problem management. Problem management is a process which the client should insist on, and keep a close eye on – direct measurement may not be easy, but the reduction in incidents for a given service should be more so.

For the outsourced service provider parent organisation, one element often missing is the meta-level problem management to identify common problems across multiple clients and, where this is missing, can result in fixes being developed in silos, resulting in waste and squandered learning.

Configuration management is the second process that is likely to be agreed contractually and not implemented effectively. Frequently configuration management is seen as a 'background' process and therefore a cost by the service provider, and one that is not directly measurable. This is a big mistake: without configuration management, all the operational processes listed above are more expensive to carry out and overall control of services is much weakened. Configuration management tells the provider what the overall service looks like, what the components are, how they interact – it gives the ability to manage the service. Without configuration management, support teams are often shooting in the dark.

The client needs to ensure that promises to deliver configuration management are met and, again, this needs to be closely watched so that a spreadsheet listing the servers used (for example) is not presented as being a configuration management system – which it is not! One of the commonest problems with configuration processes is that the quality of data; inventory and records, is frequently compromised by the need for a client service provider to keep contract lifecycle costs to a minimum, or simply a lack of effective data quality governance, creating problems for not just one but many of a service provider's clients.

Capacity management is a key sister process to availability management and allows for planning and the prevention of performance deterioration. It is not just the ongoing measurement of capacity for reporting purposes, but should be used to drive intervention before capacity limits are met. Poor capacity management results in failures in availability and performance for the client and excessive costs for service providers.

Good tools and automation allow availability, capacity and performance monitoring to be carried out largely resource-independently. They also allow integration to the service level management process allowing low-cost, high-quality reporting. Automated monitoring allows events to be detected and pro-actively managed – and the automatic creation of incidents and provision of data for problems.

All outsource providers use tools, but they are not all as integrated as they could be, nor are they always set up to do all the things that are needed. It is up to the client to ensure that the provider is doing all they can in this respect. Further, this is another area where bespoke requirements, such as non-standard operating systems on servers, can have a major impact on the automation capability.

Missing processes

Non-standard request fulfilment – one of the key missing ITIL processes – is frequently missing from contract implementation. Where this is the case there is a tendency for non-standard requests to all go through the project route, and in this case the cost of fulfilling the requests is very frequently more than their value. They can also escape from the constraints of a contract if they were not anticipated and this can also cause dissent and disagreement between client and service provider, as well as resulting in escalating costs for demand that doesn't easily fit into unsuitable categories or processes.

Asset/software lifecycle management is also underemphasised in ITIL: It should be obvious that stocks need refreshing, that hardware and software versions need updating and that, sometimes, technologies need replacing. However, although it is rare for all of these to be missed, it does happen. Ensuring that there are clear processes for doing this can reduce problems in the medium and long term.

Process issues can be much reduced if:

- The underlying processes with the potential to support the 'frontline' processes are given sufficient resource and focus – principally configuration management, problem management and event management (including monitoring tooling).

- Change management is used effectively to protect the live environment from unauthorised changes.

- Non-standard request processes are built into the contract, especially where ITIL and other frameworks lack useful guidelines.

- Outsource providers reuse process content, rather than re-inventing them for each contract, since reuse enables deployment of common support applications and reduces unnecessary costs.

This is more likely to happen if the outsourced service provider's service manager – the owner of all these processes – is fully qualified in ITIL (or a similar) process methodology and understands the relationships between processes. Having a similar responsibility in the client organisation can make sure that this happens.

Organisational problems – *of the first kind*

Outsourced organisations suffer from all the organisational issues raised in Chapter 6 regarding the various options for structuring. Depending on the shape of the outsourced IT account and the priorities given to various features, there will always be areas of weakness. This is inevitable and needs active management based on the understanding obtained from an investigation similar to that outlined in Chapter 6.

Additionally, within each part of the organisation and also applying to the whole of the outsourced account, problems arise when the outsourced IT is not structured according to the systems described in the previous section.

Ironically, these problems occur most frequently when the focus of the outsourced IT leadership team is on the client – perhaps because they are firefighting or maybe because they have a sales mentality, either from natural preference or from corporate policy and incentive. There is not enough time available to spend all one's time in client meetings and to try to manage a failing organisation.

A vicious circle can occur here – poor organisation results in occasional but serious issues that come to the attention of the client; the client demands more of the leadership's attention in meetings and managing remediation; the leadership have less time to manage the IT outsourced organisation; the poor organisation results in more, occasional but serious, issues.

Failures in the *innovation* system normally arise in the improvement area – especially when the attention is on firefighting problems.

These organisation failings can largely be avoided if:

- The outsourced service provider focuses on effective governance in all these areas.

- Client/outsource governance meetings take place at all levels in the organisation (ladder governance – see below).

- Escalation routes are clear for all processes – in the client and the outsourced service provider.

- Regular meetings are scheduled with pre-agreed agendas and structured management information available to review.

- There are clear and interlocking roles and responsibilities for all staff – not in too much detail, the emphasis is on clarity – and these are used in management.

- There is a regular pattern and sequence of meetings and informal networks up and down, and across the organisation so that problems are resolved at the appropriate level, and without having to escalate everything.

- Clear decisions are taken, documented and followed through.

- Resource is allocated to fixing the organisation – staff won't do it in their spare time!

- Outsource leadership allocates time to walk about and find out what is really going on.

- Outsource leadership avoids being pulled into endless meetings with the client – if necessary delegate these meetings or, if not possible, delegate the management of the outsource organisation.

- A proper management system is consciously built, based on a model of the organisation that is commonly understood; not just a quality system in a specialised ghetto, but one that everyone recognises and uses.

- Proper mechanisms are designed for upwards feedback; ones that utilise walk-about contact, but also create other opportunities for the ideas and frustrations of staff to be heard.

Behind these fixes is a bigger one – the outsourced service provider should appoint someone or even a team to own the organisational system – governance, operating model and processes as well. This team may be in the architect groups or part of the improvement activity and can ensure that all the important systems are in place.

Chapter 7 – Outsourcing the Service

Organisational problems – *of the second kind*

"The unit lead seems to have her own agenda and regularly misses account board meetings. Her communications go out without reference to or agreement from other account leaders. She only gets really involved when the allocation of profits to the solution groups is discussed.

"Staff working on the account can seem rudderless and demotivated because their team leader is remote and otherwise engaged. The different solution groups use their own reporting tools, making it hard to gather management information for the account leader. It doesn't feel as though the account is pulling together."

This second type of problem arises when the outsourced IT is not structured according to the client but to the internal structure of the outsource parent organisation.

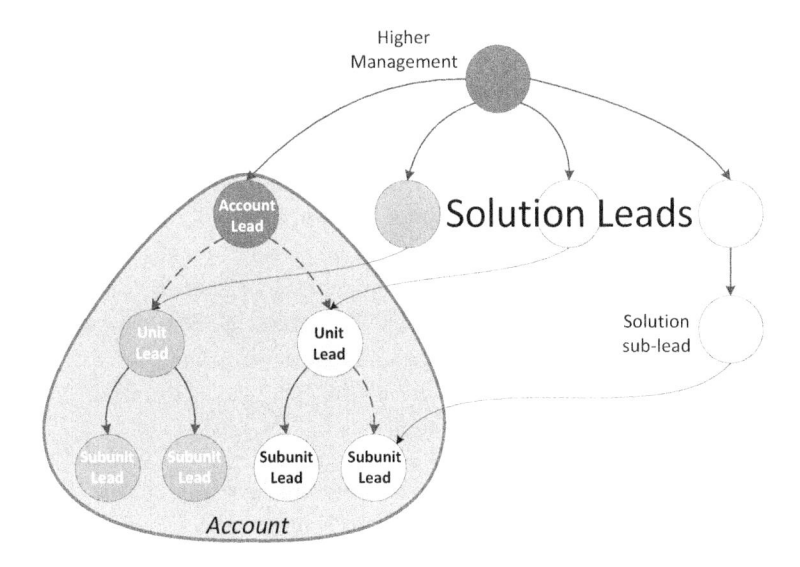

Figure 7.5 The outsourced service provider organises solutions centrally and does not give the account lead any line authority over staff resource – even when they are operating within her/his account.

Outsource suppliers tend to be structured to provide bespoke services to large clients or vanilla services to a range of clients. This point was made at the start. Again, these are extremes and many fall between these.

Reframing ITIL

The bespoke service provider usually has the outsource supplier structured principally by 'account' – i.e. client. At the extreme, each client has a dedicated account organisation which manages all the staff servicing that client. The benefit here is that each client gets a highly dedicated service; the weakness is that it is difficult for the outsource supplier to get economies of scale, to have flexibility in staff allocation, to provide access to the latest developments or to ensure consistency of approach and delivery. However, from an organisational point of view this structure is relatively straightforward as the structure simply (!) needs to follow the guidelines of organisational systems as detailed above.

The provision of vanilla services is also relatively straightforward. In this case the outsource supplier does not provide a client-based organisational structure at all, but organises itself on a technical, geographical or some other basis. The client focus is provided by some form of business relationship manager whose role is to ensure that the vanilla services on offer meet the client needs and to deal with any issues arising. In reality this becomes an almost impossible role as the supplier's vanilla service nearly always gets modified for the client, and the organisational structure struggles to manage this; the more diverse the clients, their size, sectors and demands, the worse this becomes.

The vast majority of client-outsourced service provider relationships, and hence outsourced service provider organisational structures lie in between these two extremes. This may mean that the need for the account to provide a viable organisation which can meet the bespoke client needs is compromised by the outsource suppliers 'centralised' organisation. Hence the staff who are nominally in the account actually report to someone else (in their technical, geographical or some other organisation). This makes it almost impossible for the account leaders to control or even influence the performance of the operational staff – with inevitable consequences.

Another complication is that the account leadership team may include 'leaders' of operational staff who don't report to the account leader in any other respect and who behave with a degree of independence and autonomy that can be damaging to consistent development and delivery of an account strategy.

To put it simple, the account is operationally and managerially neither fish nor fowl; its purpose is unclear and the result is confusion, demotivation and poor customer service.

Chapter 7 – Outsourcing the Service

These problems can be reduced if:

- The outsourced service provider has a clear view of which organisational model it is following and the consequences.

- The outsourced service provider considers alternative models of delivery and adopts one or the other depending on the size and nature of a contract.

- Clear indirect routes to manage performance are developed and used when direct management responsibility for operational staff on the account is not with the account leadership.

- Clear organisational accountability for delivery is established as the delivery model is developed, and then regularly reviewed during the lifecycle of the contract.

- The client has identified how the outsourced service provider intends to resource and control the resources in a contract, before it is signed.

The benefits of 'economies of scale' in IT are more often mythical than real. This is not made easier by the difficulty of measuring productivity in the IT sphere. It is highly possible that an 'account' model for medium and large accounts, using staff contracted-in from 'capability homes' and reporting to the account management for the duration, provides not only the best client service, but also a cost-effective solution.

The relationship

Although it is not unheard of for the client organisation to have just a skeleton team receiving management information from an outsourced service provider, it is rare for this structure to survive. More typically, contracts specify a series of governance boards which may be specified to review so many reports that, where they to do it conscientiously, would mean the participants spending all day every day in such meetings!

Additionally, most contracts start off on the wrong foot. To win a contract the outsource provider frequently has to offer a price that often leaves the contract breaking even or perhaps making a loss. The aim is to make up for this by selling-on additional services, however, the effect this selling has on the client is to reduce trust. Frequently, there is little understanding of the time lags and

Reframing ITIL

causal relationships between an initial sale, incremental sales, gross margin at point of sale, subsequent cost of sales, and expected contract profit expectations at various stages of the contract's lifecycle.

Should any large failure occur – in the technical service or the business processes – it provides a strong motivator for the frequent review of performance and management information. The outsource service provider's leadership team can rapidly find themselves in crisis meetings and spending large amounts of time and money in remediation projects. This occurs because the governance structures have been unable to prevent the dissatisfaction and failures at an earlier stage.

Trust has vanished and increasingly onerous controls are put in place, the client recruits staff whose main role is to keep an eye on the outsourcer – costs start to rocket. In addition, costs of failure, service recovery and goodwill mitigation with clients are very often poorly understood, if not hidden altogether from financial scrutiny.

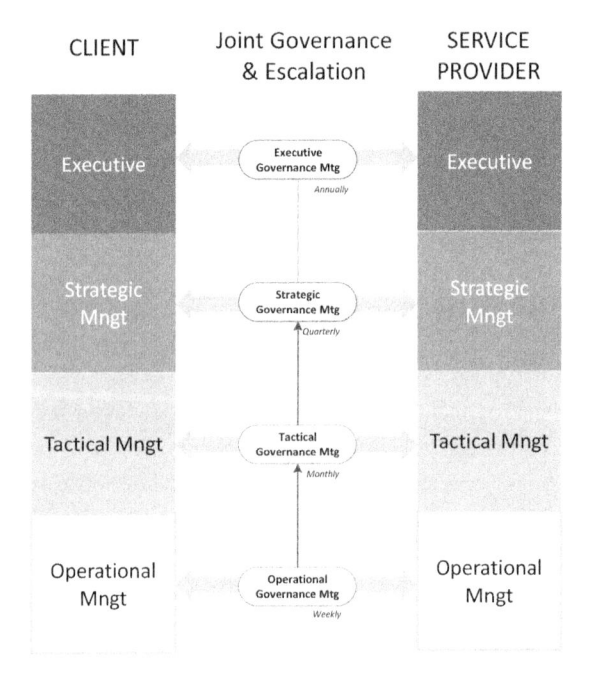

Figure 7.6 Ladder governance allows issues to be resolved at the lowest possible level and only issues that cannot be so resolved are escalated to higher rungs on the governance ladder

Chapter 7 – Outsourcing the Service

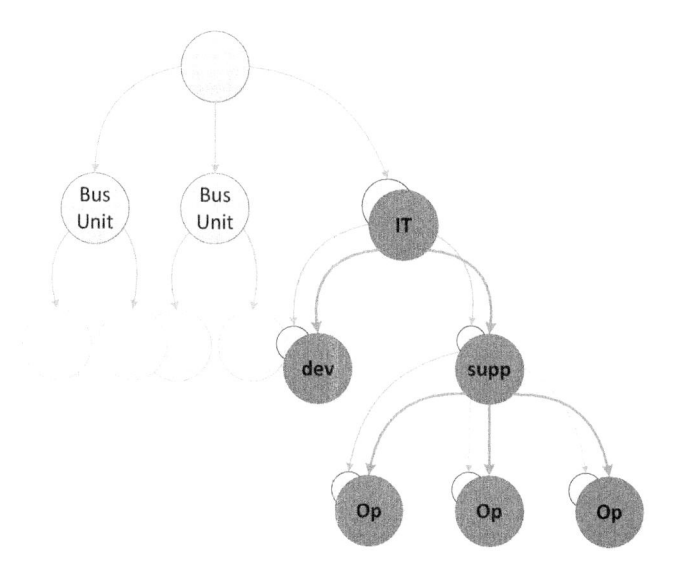

Figure 7.7 The outsourced IT organisation has a shadowed client organisation that mirrors much of its structure. The sizes of the shadow groups can vary from negligible to almost marking the outsourced organisation head for head – not an efficient use of resources

If all this can be pre-empted it leads to a much happier and successful relationship. The contract may be used to define a ladder governance structure – client roles are created to mirror each layer in the IT support organisation. Their function is to ensure that processes are followed, performance meets expectations and management is effective. They meet regularly with their peers where they review only the appropriate amount of information. Concerns are escalated and so the senior teams become involved only if the lower rungs of the ladder have failed to resolve an issue.

Another interesting part of the client-outsourcer relationship occurs at the top level, where the old head of IT and the new outsourced IT account management team operate. The relationship here is what glues the outsourced IT department into the client organisation.

We can consider elements of this relationship within the level of management by using the organisational systems frame we used in Chapters 4, 5 and the section above.

Reframing ITIL

As in the other diagrams showing the two organisations, the lighter shading here represents the client organisation and darker shading the outsourced IT provider. The proportion of activity/influence of each of these organisations as shown here and described immediately below is only an example: it could be very different.

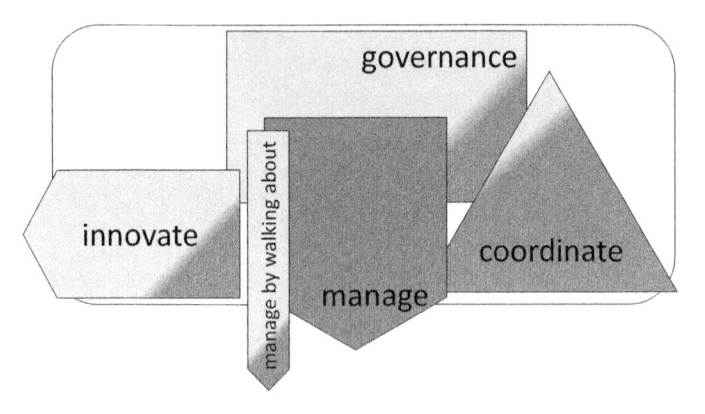

Figure 7.8 Example of the split between the proportions of each organisational system managed by the client (lighter shading) or the outsource provider (darker shading) shown in the organisational systems frame.

In the example shown in Figure 7.8, the client organisation has taken the leading role in *governance* – this really shows the balance of power in the new IT organisation. Also the client has taken the lead in directing *innovation*; in other cases the outsourced provider might be asked/expected to provide the initiatives and ideas here. *Coordination* – providing standards and practices is managed principally by the outsourced provider through ITIL and their automated processes; in this case the client coordinates the management of the relationship.

Perhaps not surprisingly, the outsourced provider has taken the full role of *managing* the staff and their activities and formal reporting of progress, but the client has taken a significant role in checking that what the client tells them is happening is actually happening (*management by walking about*).

Organisational cultures

And almost finally, the least ITIL-related issue, but a key one for the relationship is the culture of the two organisations involved: It can often seem that the two new partners – the client and the outsource provider – seem to be

Chapter 7 – Outsourcing the Service

at cross purposes, with different expectations. It is as if they spoke different languages.

In reality of course, they do – not based on their nationality but on their cultures. Different organisations can have very difference cultures – in the form of terminology, behaviours, standards, quality, structures etc. This often comes as a surprise, as it can be very hard to imagine how a different organisation might be if you have not worked at various levels in the hierarchy of several different ones.

There are often different expectations of quality systems – for example in the level of record keeping, minute taking, documentation, approval mechanisms, and care in following standards.

There may be differences in communication style – the nature and frequency of meetings, amount of honesty in communications (e.g. *does 'yes' mean 'yes', or 'maybe'?)*, willingness to accept suggestions up the hierarchy, professionalism of communication material or the commitment to speak with 'one voice'. When a deadline or target is set, is this a commitment, or is it something that can largely be allowed to pass without any great surprise or concern?

Even more serious are deeper issues – how hierarchical a business is, the willingness of managers and staff to take criticism, the level of honesty expected in appraisals, the use or otherwise of 360 feedback and mechanisms for continuous improvement.

If there is an assumption that some or all of these will be the same in the outsourced service provider as in the client, then the client is likely to be in for a rude shock! Many of these misalignments can give rise to major issues – especially in the early days and years – for any transitioned staff, for the expectations of the outsourcing client, and for the client's customers.

If organisations are different in these aspects – and they will be – then it is unlikely that either organisation would be able to change. However, awareness of these issues can at least anticipate the problems they may cause.

Some of these points are so serious that they really should be addressed in the contract, although it is rare for this to be the case. To make sure these are addressed, due diligence should be carried out by the client – who may wish to employ a third party with particular expertise in this area. In this way, expectations can be clarified and where appropriate, the client expectations documented.

Service/operational integration (SIAM)

Service Integration and Management (SIAM) – not systems integration and management which is a different thing entirely – is now a well-established approach with its own guidance. We do not attempt to do other than give a very basic explanation of how this works here.

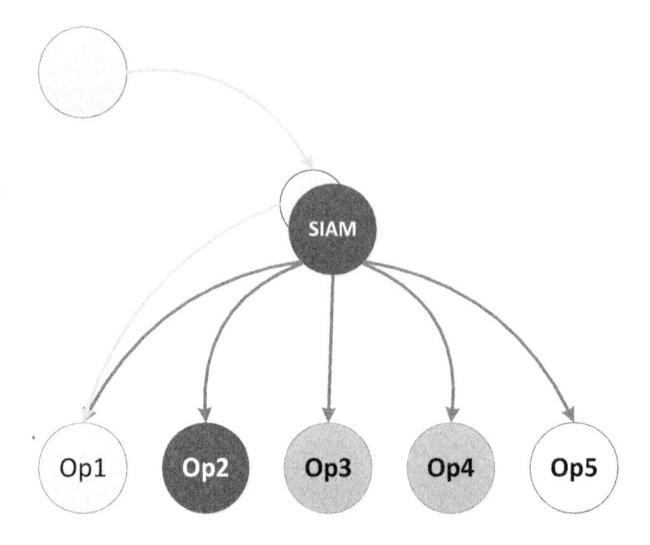

Figure 7.9 Service management organisation with a lead supplier as service integrator

A SIAM based outsource is where a third-party 'management' service integrator is given the role of managing a number of outsource service providers on behalf of the client. Not uncommonly the service providers may include client departments and other departments of the service integrator business. Both these options are shown in Figure 7.9. Each shade of grey represents a different organisation.

The example shown in Figure 7.9 is an example of a lead supplier as service integrator. Other structures include the client as service integrator, an independent external service integrator and hybrid service integrator (where the client and a lead service integrator jointly manage SIAM).

Chapter 7 – Outsourcing the Service

The client organisation has an executive above the IT level, a residual IT management group managing the contract and keeping an eye on the outsourcers, and also a single IT service (Op1) – which could be development, local area networks, applications, almost anything. The business providing the SIAM management team here also provides one of the IT services – Op2. Two other outsource businesses provide one (Op5) and two (Op3 and Op4) services respectively. Ideally, the SIAM group and the Op2 service provider group should be separated by 'internal walls' in their parent outsource business.

The approach used in Figure 7.8 can also be applied here to the SIAM organisation. Sometimes separate diagrams can be produced for each of the ITIL processes – e.g. a problem management process may be coordinated by the client; the availability management processes may be devolved to the lower level service providers; incident management may be actually *managed* by the SIAM group ...and so forth.

Using the organisational system frame, the specific roles of the SIAM group can be categorised and understood. This understanding, shared between the participating parties can smooth the processes and relationships between otherwise competing entities.

There are many other areas that provide problems in the SIAM structure. For example, it is not uncommon for the SIAM provider to also provide a common service desk. If this is to provide any first-time fixes it needs access to knowledge originating with all the service providers. This introduces ownership of intellectual property (IP) problems.

The problems of coordinating an end-to-end, even seamless set of services in the structure are considerable and require considerable expertise.

Summary

IT services may be offered through a range of organisational models. The simplest is still undoubtedly the 'in-house' IT department. Relationships in this case are all internal to the organisation, although placing IT departments in separate parts of the organisation to those they are serving is perhaps an inevitable complicating factor.

For outsourced IT services, the simplest arrangement is where vanilla services are outsourced as services and the outsourcer delivers them at arms' length, without setting up a specific account for the client. In this case a client service manager is responsible for the relationship. Nonetheless, expectations and actual deliverables still provide sources of conflict.

Once an account specific to a client is established, many organisational problems begin to arise and these are discussed above. Further complications can be introduced for large IT services when multiple outsource providers are involved. The SIAM model attempts to, and goes some way to, mediating these.

Overall, these complications can best be understood from a systems thinking perspective – especially using the viable system model. We believe this to be a universal frame which can help in many situations and hope you will also find it so in practical applications.

Chapter 8

Summary

Visualisation of ITIL

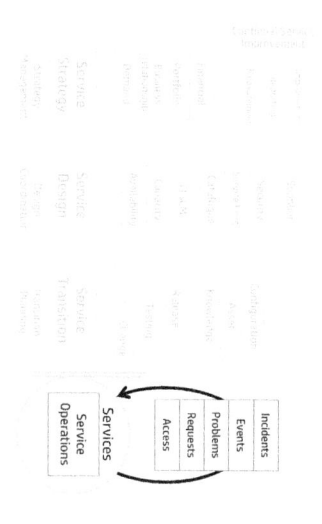

Chapters 1 & 2 – Support Operations processes

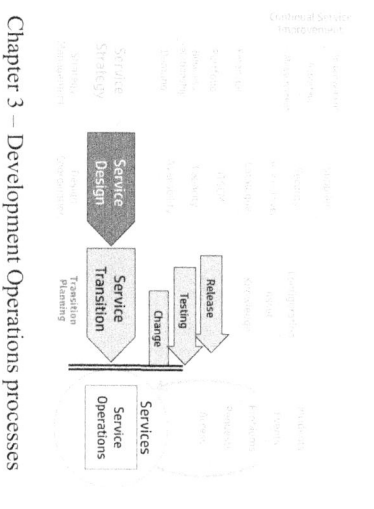

Chapter 3 – Development Operations processes

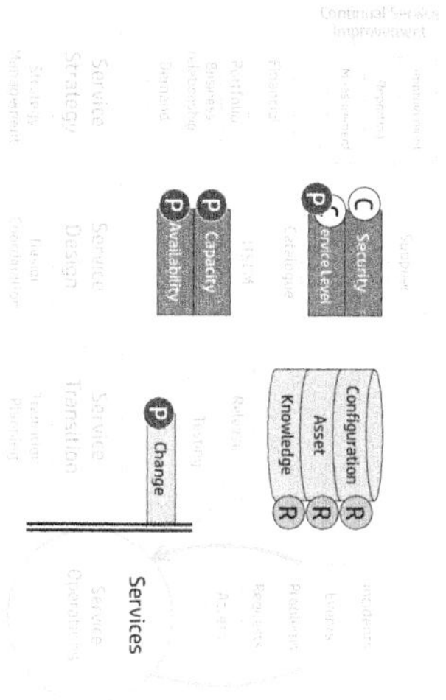

Chapter 4 – Managing the Service processes

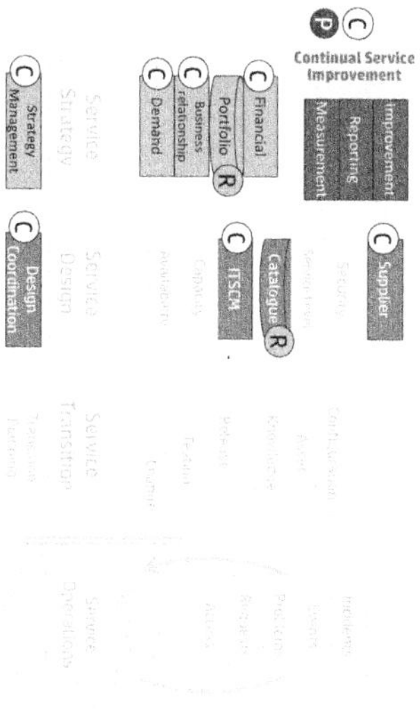

Chapter 5 – Managing the service organisation processes

Reframing ITIL

Figure 8.1 The ITIL frame – Chapters 1-5 *(see previous page)*

We started in Chapter 1 with a visualisation of ITIL 3 – as the main version of ITIL currently in use. This showed the ITIL processes grouped together and partly characterised as processes (P), capabilities (C) or repositories (R). As grouped by chapter, this looks like the figure above (Figure 8.1).

This set the context of each investigation and, if anything, showed how different the systems-thinking framing of ITIL was. Clearly if we had set ITIL 2 or 4 as the baseline this would have looked different, however, it is only to set context. The main point is that the five ITIL 3 disciplines don't logically map onto the organisational processes except Service Operation – which is where it all started. This is revisited again at the end of this summary.

Cybernetic loops and flows

In Chapter 1 we looked at the Service Operation processes: incidents, problems and requests, and framed them as cybernetic loops. In doing this it became apparent that some important loops/processes were missing: in particular non-standard requests and the lifecycle management processes. This let us identify some problems this can cause and how to remedy them. CSI was also identified as a cousin of the problem management process.

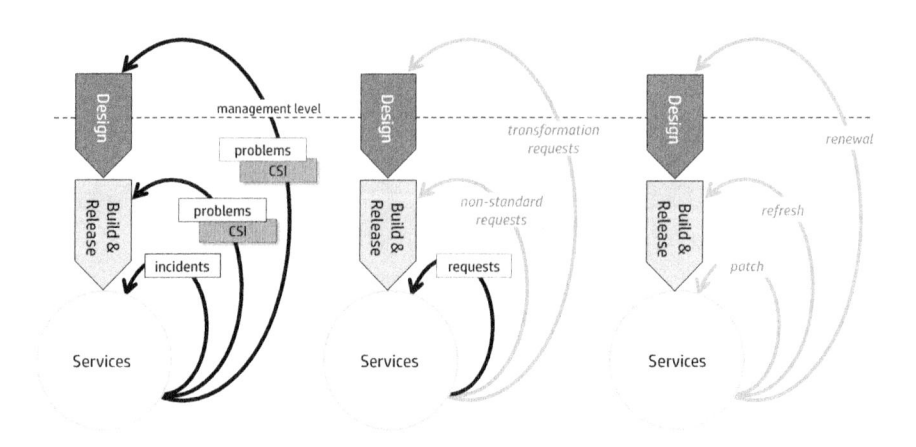

Figure 8.2 Chapter 1 – The Service Management process loops

Chapter 8 – Summary

Loop Type	Characteristics	Troubleshoot/ Operational Control	Request Fulfilment	Service Lifecycle Management
		Failure Driven	User Driven	Supplier Driven
Stability	high volume, low value, quick	Incidents	Standard Requests/ Access Mngt	Patching & Stock Mngt
Adaptability	medium volume, medium value, medium timescale	Problems	Non-Standard Requests	End-of-life, Refresh
Transformation	low volume, high value, long timescale	Problems	Transformation Requests	Renewal Programmes

Table 8.1   Chapter 1 – Characteristics of the Service Management process loops

Chapter 2 took the investigation of support operations processes further and showed how these processes are managed in a very simple organisation and how the process flows for incidents and requests move between different operational departments. Service desks were also introduced and their value and issues shown.

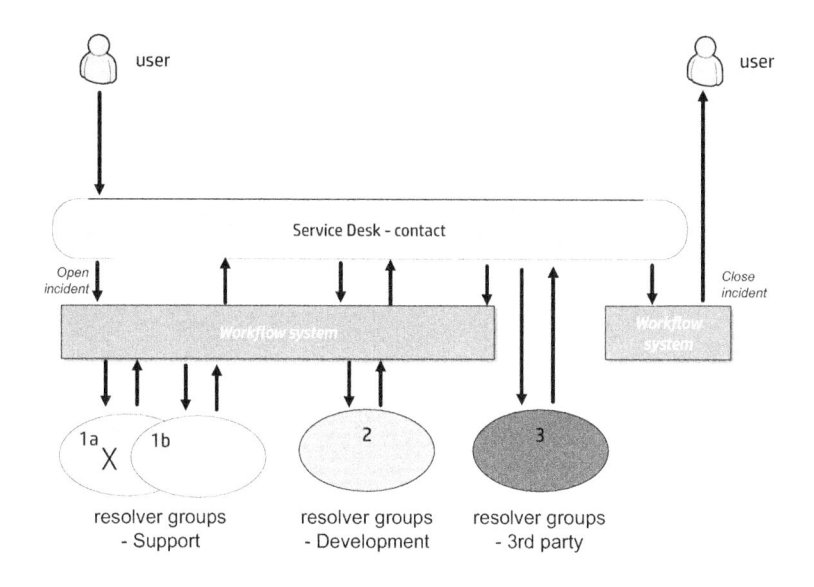

Figure 8.3   Chapter 2 – Flow diagram showing typical resource used in incident management

155

Reframing ITIL

Development and Transition

Chapter 3 looked at the issues in development – a large part of the largest, transformational, cybernetic loop. This addressed the release, testing and project management processes and some parts of Service Design. The particular issues of Agile and DevOps developments, rather than waterfall, were briefly highlighted.

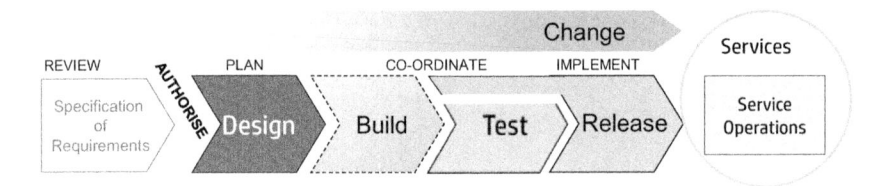

Figure 8.4   Chapter 3 – ITIL processes in service development

Chapter 3 also introduced the communications frame and considered intra-project communication between project staff of different stages, extra-project communication – mainly with the client and inter-project communication – between projects. The problems of inter-project communication were considered based on the number of dependencies introduced by large numbers of projects and how to reduce them with programmes.

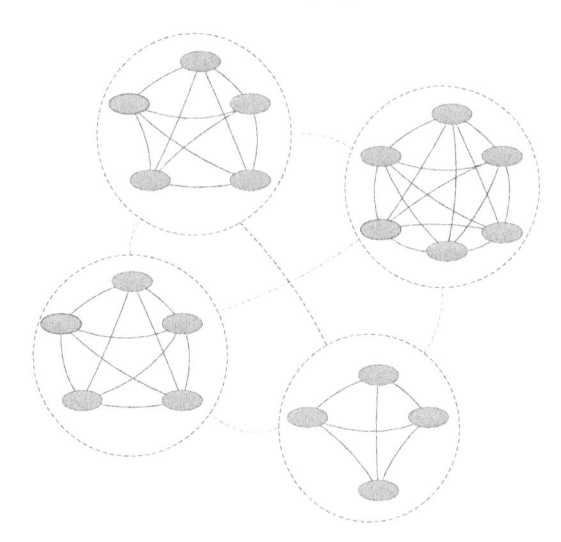

Figure 8.5   Chapter 3 – Reducing the number of interactions between twenty projects by grouping into programmes

Viable systems

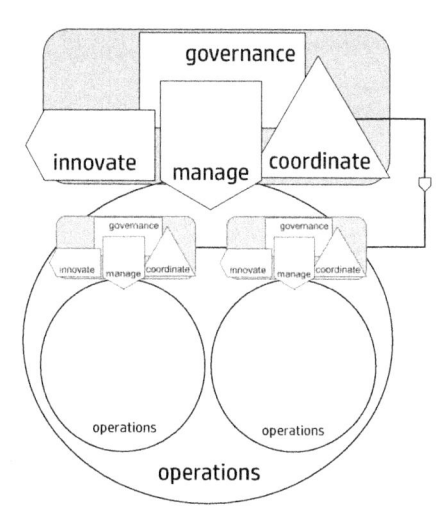

Figure 8.6 Chapter 4 & 5 – Detail of management processes in the viable system frame

Chapters 4 & 5 introduced the viable system frame – as being the best model for looking at organisational activities – and its management and operational systems. This was then used to characterise the remaining ITIL processes – process by process – to see which of the systems each covers.

This was done at two levels in the organisation – the service level (Chapter 4) and the service organisation level (Chapter 5).

It showed that ITIL does contain all the elements necessary to provide a viable system – but only if all are implemented. This is rare, especially with the more business focused processes where organisations understandably prefer to use their normal organisational processes. Another weakness was the lack of coverage of people and capabilities in ITIL. Integration with non-ITIL versions of alternative processes as in finance can be poor. The problems of partial implementation were discussed.

The summary frames below are shown in reverse order so that the higher level of the organisation is above:

Reframing ITIL

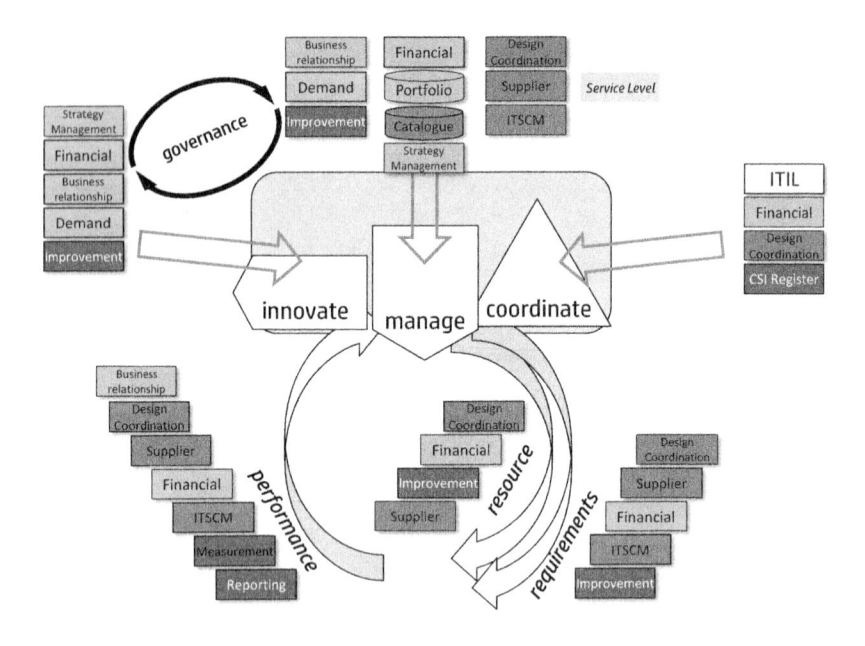

Figure 8.7   Chapter 5 – Viable system model for the whole service organisation

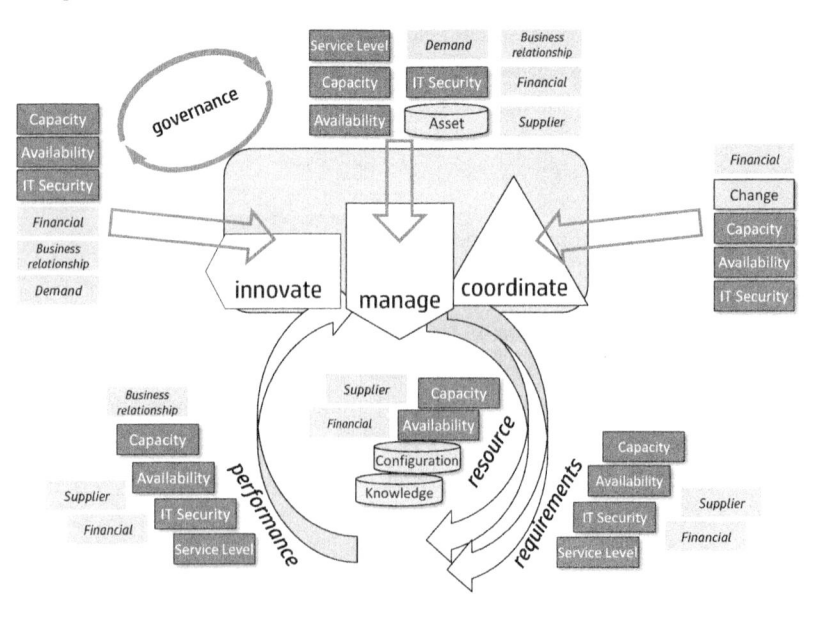

Figure 8.8   Chapter 4 – Viable system model for managing the service.
Grey, italicised boxes are inherited down from other levels – see above

Chapter 8 – Summary

Organisational issues

The blob diagram was introduced as a useful frame for considering an organisation's structure. It was stressed that this is not an organisational hierarchy.

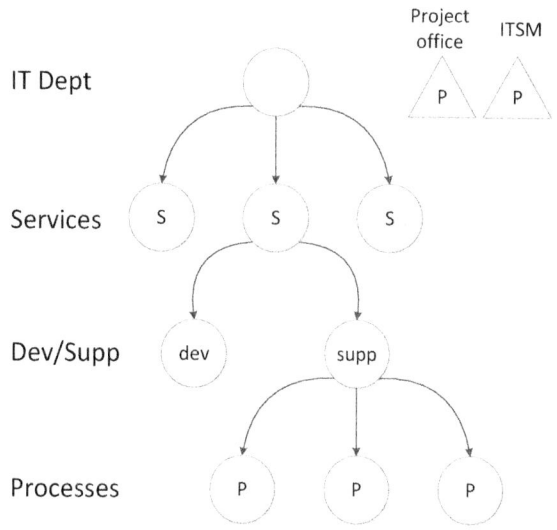

Figure 8.9   Chapter 6 – Blob diagram of the classic/simplified IT organisation

Initially, in Chapter 6, 'organisational issues of the first kind' were considered – arising from different ways of structuring an organisation.

This approach was used to look at a variety of possible structures for IT support organisations and these were compared quantitatively based on a RAYG analysis for a range of criteria. Tables were used to visualise and summarise the findings. The finding was that there are no ideal structures. The tools used allow the advantages and consequences of each organisational type to be identified showing the trade-offs of each.

Reframing ITIL

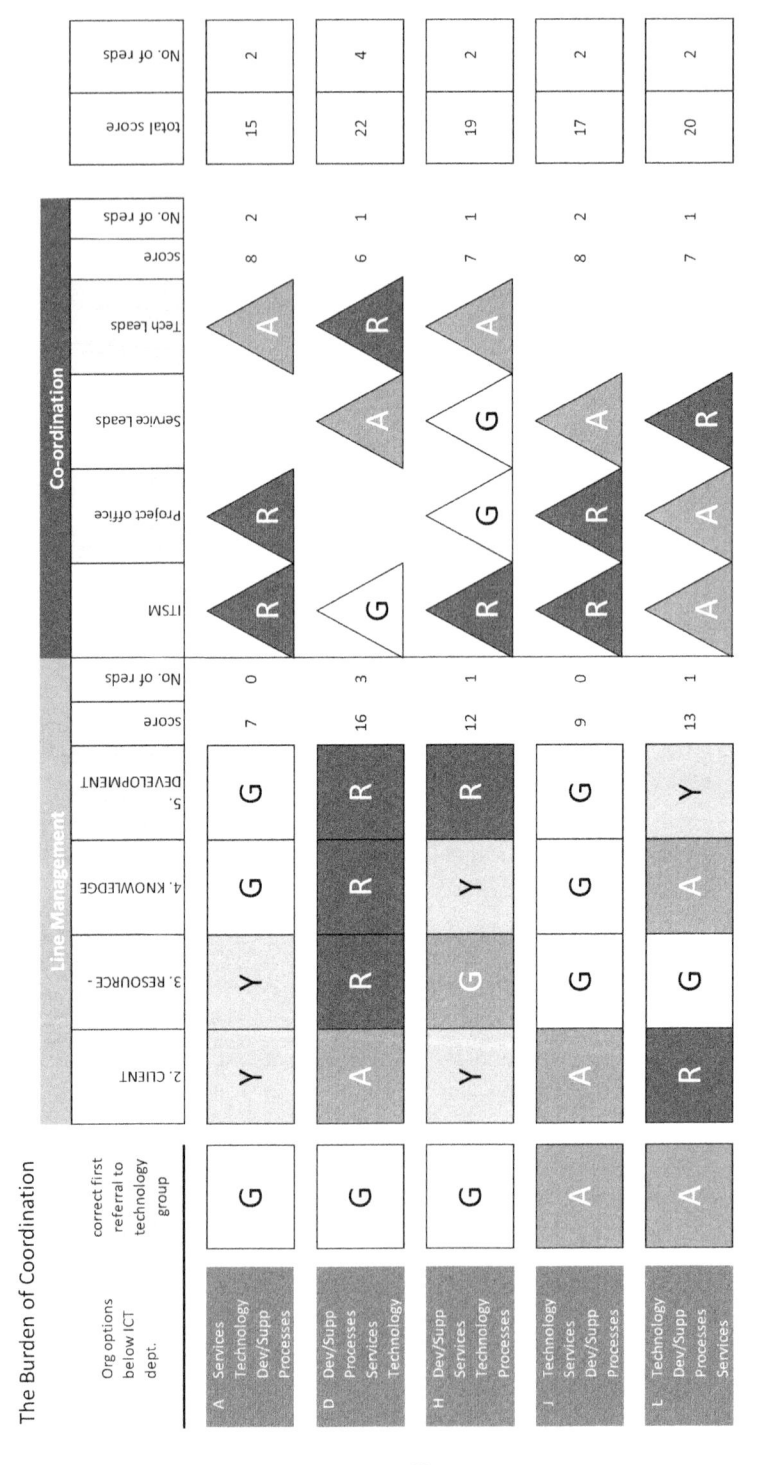

The Burden of Coordination

Org options below ICT dept.	correct first referral to technology group	2. CLIENT	3. RESOURCE	4. KNOWLEDGE	5. DEVELOPMENT	score	No. of reds	ITSM	Project office	Service leads	Tech leads	score	No. of reds	total score	No. of reds
A Services / Technology / Dev/Supp / Processes	G	Y	Y	G	G	7	0	R	R		A	8	2	15	2
D Dev/Supp / Processes / Services / Technology	G	A	R	R	R	16	3	G		A	R	6	1	22	4
H Dev/Supp / Services / Technology / Processes	G	Y	G	Y	R	12	1	R	G	G	A	7	1	19	2
J Technology / Services / Dev/Supp / Processes	A	A	G	G	G	9	0	R	R	A		8	2	17	2
L Technology / Dev/Supp / Processes / Services	A	R	G	A	Y	13	1	A	A	R		7	1	20	2

Line Management | Co-ordination

Table 8.2   Chapter 6 – RAYG assessments of selected organisational options including coordination options and incorporating a service desk

Chapter 8 – Summary

In Chapter 7 a variety of frames were introduced for looking particularly at outsourced IT support organisations. Standardised vs bespoke outsourcing was considered.

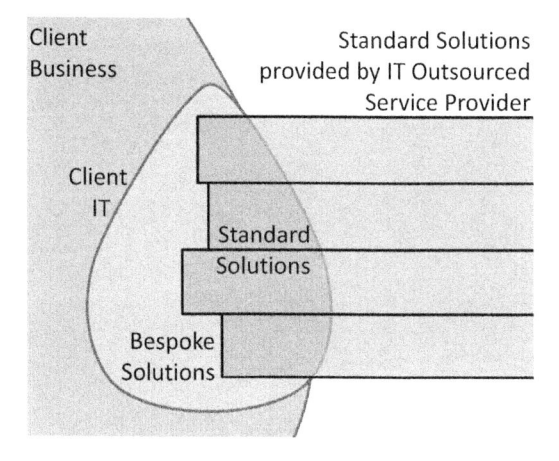

Figure 8.10   Chapter 7 – The standard solutions provided by the IT outsourced service provider cannot fill the needs of the client IT. There is still a gap that requires some bespoke solutions, even if not described as such

The idea of partial implementation was revisited as were the viable system model (VSM) 'systems'. The 'blob' frame was now used to consider indirect management and the problems it causes.

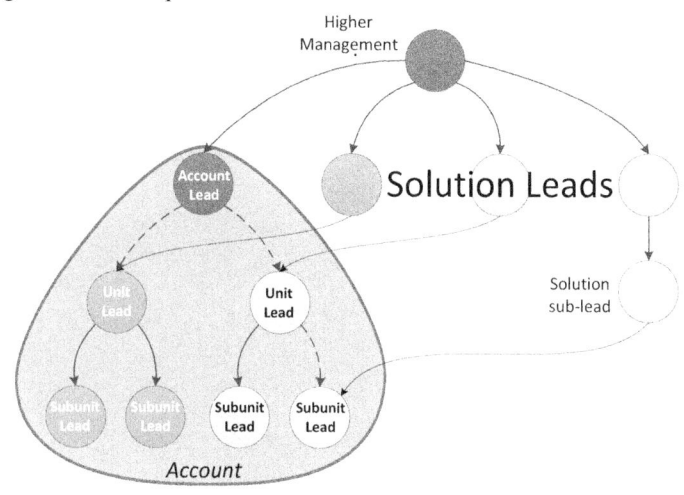

Figure 8.11   Chapter 7 – The outsource service provider organises solutions centrally and does not give the account lead any line authority over them – even when they are operating within their account

Reframing ITIL

Relationship and contracts were discussed and the frame of ladder governance.

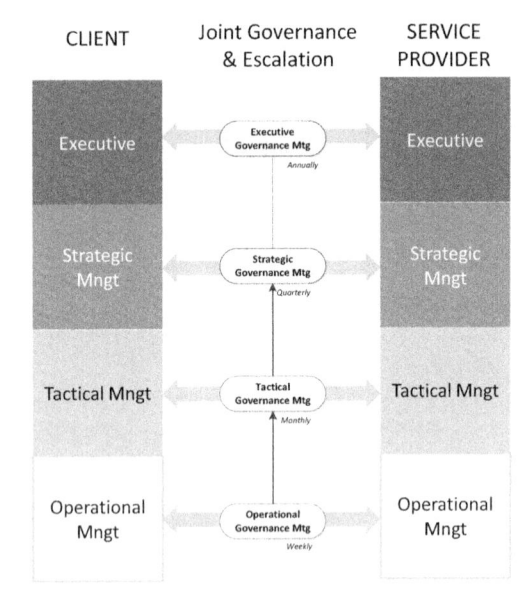

Figure 8.12 Chapter 7 – Ladder governance allows issues to be resolved at the lowest possible level and only issues that cannot be so resolved are escalated to higher rungs on the governance ladder

Finally, multi-supplier outsourcing using a Service Integration and Management (SIAM) model was briefly introduced.

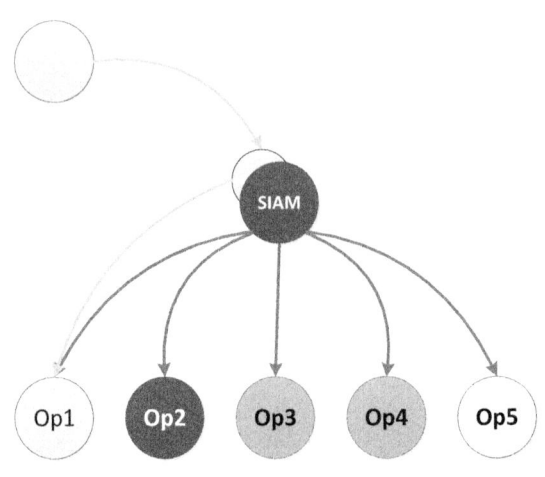

Figure 8.13 Chapter 7 – Service management organisation with a lead supplier as service integrator

Chapter 8 – Summary

In Chapter 7 the approach throughout was how to solve the problems introduced.

Grouping ITIL processes

Figure 8.1 at the start of this summary chapter began to introduce the idea that ITIL processes could be grouped differently from the approaches used in ITIL 2 and 3 (& 4).

Using the systems thinking approach we have applied throughout this book, the grouping looks like:

Support operations processes:
- Incident Management
- Event Management
- Problem Management
- Request Fulfilment
- Access Management

Development operations processes:
- [Service Design]
- [Obtain/build – *ITIL 4 only*]
- Test Management
- Release Management

Processes for managing the Service:
- Configuration Management
- Asset Management
- Knowledge Management
- Change Management (*incl.* Change Evaluation)
- Capacity Management
- Availability Management
- Security Management
- Service Level Management
- [Continual Service Improvement]

Processes for managing the service organisation:
- Supplier Management
- Catalogue Management
- IT Service Continuity Management
- Design Coordination
- Demand Management
- Business Relationship Management
- Strategy Management for IT Services
- Portfolio Management

This grouping is based in sound systems thinking principles but, more importantly, should make some logical sense and make it easier to remember what each process is for.

Applicability

The intention of this work was to reframe IT Service Management in IT support organisations. However, as we worked through the sections, something else emerged and led to much discussion. We began to feel that almost everything in this book could be applied to other service organisations – the NHS, vehicle servicing, banks and building societies, the railways, local government departments etc. Not just the big ideas but many of the details seemed applicable. The biggest difference seen is in the extent of the delivery group of activities which can be much bigger in these non-IT organisations. However, the differences seem to lie mainly in emphasis and terminology. We then looked further and realised that the same ideas can be applied to widget producing organisations!

The temptation to carry out a more widespread study across organisational types is considerable but has so far been resisted. So, if you feel that the insights you have from this book are useful elsewhere, please feel free to use them – and perhaps let us know how it works out.

Further Reading

System Thinking

Patrick Hoverstadt (2009) The Fractal Organization: Creating Sustainable Organizations with the Viable System Model. Wiley, 338pp, ISBN-13: 978-0470060568

Stafford Beer (1995) Heart of Enterprise (Classic Beer Series). Wiley, 600pp, ISBN-13: 978-0471948377

Christopher Alexander (1974) Notes on the Synthesis of Form. Harvard University Press, 216pp, ISBN-13: 978-0674627512

Peter Senge (2006) The Fifth Discipline: The art and practice of the learning organization. Random House Business; 2nd revised edition, 464 pp, ISBN-13: 978-1905211203

Donella Meadows (2017) Thinking in Systems: a Primer. Chelsea Green Publishing Co., 240pp, ISBN-13: 978-1603580557

Learning, change and knowledge

Chris Argyris (1999) On Organizational Learning. Wiley-Blackwell; 2nd edition, 480 pp, ISBN-13: 978-0631213093

Max Boisot (1994) Information and Organizations: The Manager as Anthropologist, HarperCollins, ASIN: B01LPDBWCK

Max Boisot (1999) Knowledge Assets: Securing Competitive Advantage in the Information Economy. Oxford University Press, ASIN: B00LY0ZO5G

Patrick Hoverstadt (2005) Mosaic Transformation in Organisations. in *Organisational Transformation and Social Change*

Masaaki Imai (1988) Kaizen: The key to Japan's competitive success. McGraw-Hill; 260 pp, ISBN-13: 978-0075543329

Kaoru Ishikawa (1985) What is Total Quality Control?: The Japanese Way. Prentice Hall; ASIN: B0161THGD2

Joseph M Juran and A Blanton Godfrey (1999) Juran's Quality Handbook. McGraw-Hill; 5th edition 1872 pp, ISBN-13: 978-0070340039

Project and programme management
Managing Successful Projects with PRINCE2 (May 2017) The Stationery Office; 6th edition, 425pp, ISBN-13: 978-0113315338

Managing Successful Programmes (MSP) (Aug 2011) The Stationery Office; 4th edition, 276pp, ISBN-13: 978-0113313273

Gene Kim, Patrick Debois and John Willis (Author) (2016) The DevOps Handbook: How to Create World-Class Agility, Reliability, and Security in Technology Organizations. Trade Select, 250pp, ISBN-13: 978-1942788003

Jim Highsmith (2009) Agile Project Management: Creating Innovative Products (Agile Software Development). Addison-Wesley Professional; 2nd edition, 424pp, ISBN-13: 978-0321658395

ITIL 3
ITIL foundation handbook (Jan 2012) The Stationery Office; 3rd edition, 310 pp, ISBN-13: 978-0113313495

ITIL Service Operation (Jul 2011) The Stationery Office; 2nd edition, 381pp, ISBN-13: 978-0113313075

ITIL Service Transition (Jul 2011) The Stationery Office; 2nd edition, 360pp, ISBN-13: 978-0113313068

ITIL Service Design (Jul 2011) The Stationery Office; 2nd edition, 456pp, ISBN-13: 978-0113313051

ITIL Service Strategy (Jul 2011) The Stationery Office; 2nd edition, 469pp, ISBN-13: 978-0113313044

ITIL Continual Service Improvement (Jul 2011) The Stationery Office; 2011 edition, 260pp, ISBN-13: 978-0113313082

ITIL 4
ITIL foundation (Feb 2019) The Stationery Office; ITIL 4 edition, 212 pp, ISBN-13: 978-0113316076

SIAM

Peter Wiggers, Dave Armes, Niklas Engelhart and Peter McKenzie (2015) SIAM: Principles and Practices for Service Integration and Management. Van Haren Publishing, 224pp, ISBN-13: 978-9401800259

Claire Agutter (2017) Service Integration and Management Foundation Body of Knowledge. van Haren Publishing, 200pp, ISBN-13: 978-9401801027

Printed in Great Britain
by Amazon